THOUGHTS

in

Flight

A Collection of the Works of
Carolyn Ruth Dalman Bouman Bakcr

"If I could harness my thoughts in flight
Metered and rhymed and set just right,
What a fantastic poet I would be,
Polished and published for all to see!
Imagine that."

CONTENTS

FOREWORD - MAY 2, 2021

What an immense privilege it was to have been handed a duffle bag full of Carolyn's compositions, and family photographs! From intimate letters, to memoires, to poetry, compiling this book has been a treat, and a great honor.

These works of Carolyn's were taken from both handwritten pages as well as typewritten pages. Having only been a member of the family since 2003, I may have made some mistakes with a name or place that was hard to read on a faded page. Please forgive any errors, but bring my attention to them for correction in any future printing. This book contains the materials exactly written by Carolyn, to the best of our ability. I say "our" because in full disclosure, I had the help of a young schoolteacher by the name of Brandon Hirtz. Thank you, Brandon, for your 20 hours of typing! God bless you as you join the Army.

In addition to presenting Carolyn's works in formal published format, which she would have no doubt been thrilled to see, photocopies of many pages that were in Carolyn's own handwriting are included as an Appendix, to end the book with her own warmest, most personal touch.

All of the writings and pictures in this book can be found in PDF e-book format, at the web site: www.CarolynRuthDalman.com. Feel free to share the site with extended family, friends, and fans of Carolyn. Much of the content of this book you may have read before, especially the chapter "Family Fun," as those stories had been previously compiled into a booklet by Carolyn herself. As you read this book, dear family, if you realize that a work that is in your possession has been omitted, please send me a copy. I will upload it to the website. If it turns out that there are several works not contained herein, I will print an updated version of the hardcopy book. It would be magnificent to have an "unabridged" anthology!

Carolyn's generation is known as "The Greatest Generation," and Carolyn stands out as a shining example of how exceptional that generation was. I will let her works speak for herself, and only say that from the day I met her as her new daughter-in-law, I came away with a deep appreciation for this precious soul. From her creative mind, to her caring heart, to her witty sense of humor, she was a masterpiece of God. May these, her "harnessed thoughts," inspire her prodigy.

Special thanks to Lynda and Susie for entrusting me with this collection. I'm blessed to have you as sisters-in-law. (This compilation would have been finished much sooner had I not cried through the whole thing.) Greetings and love to Dan, the rugged outdoorsman. Sam is in our hearts. And of course, abundant thanks and love to my husband Jack, for inviting me into this wonderful family. I love you all!

Yours,

Mindy Vance Bouman

CHAPTER ONE:

Chronicles of Family & Friends

October 6, 1922

October 6, 1922 was a balmy, Indian summer day in Holland, Michigan. An early frost had caused the city's tree-lined streets to blaze with color. Autumn had arrived and winter was sure to follow. But on this day, nature granted a reprieve. The temperature was 82 degrees without a cloud in the sky. It was a perfect day for finishing the last of the fall house cleaning.

The ritual began with my dad carrying out the living room rug to air on the clothesline. The lace curtains, washed and pinned onto stretchers, were set out to dry in the sunshine. The older children were off to school. The cleaning lady had arrived, and so the day began.

My mother was a robust, determined Dutch lady, 29 years of age. She had inherited from her mother a passion for cleanliness and order. With a solution of warm water, a small amount of kerosene and furniture polish, the two ladies washed and polished to a shine all the woodwork, cleaned the windows with a vinegar and water solution, and as they were about to scrub the floors, my mother decided to take a break. Maybe she had exerted herself too much or maybe the serious accident she had witnessed from the front porch the day before had upset her more than she realized. Whatever, it was time for a breather.

She slipped into the bathroom for a five-minute break, and there, the pleasantly muffled sounds of men at work in the lumber yard across the street and the soft breeze lazily toying with the curtains, lulled her off to a nice, well-earned nap.

Suddenly, the day's agenda came to an abrupt halt. Without any warning, like a bolt out of the blue, my mother awoke to find herself in the final stages of labor for a baby two weeks early. Panicked, she yelled at the cleaning lady to close the window; she was not about to share the sounds of a woman in labor with the men across the street. The lady rushed in and she, hands dripping with Fels Naptha soap suds, was just in time to pick up their new baby girl.

3

A runner was sent for my dad. He rushed home to find everybody jubilant and all under control. They discussed the need for a doctor, but this was their sixth home birth, and they knew what to do. It was decided that a doctor was not necessary. It has given me great pleasure to know that I arrived without expense or hard labor.

The next day, it snowed. My dad, bundled up in winter clothing, rode his trusty bike to Holland City Hall to register the birth.

In due time, the birth certificate arrived from the county seat in Grand Haven, Michigan. Caroline Ruth Dalman, daughter of Gerrit Dalman and Tillie (Dykstra) Dalman, had arrived.

My Mother

My mother loved babies. She was the happiest and most energetic when pregnant, and each new baby was greeted with joy. However, by the time the little one grew to have a mind of its own, my mother was ready for another baby; and the neighbors sighed, and the teachers groaned, and the thought of my mother's continuing inspection of every activity at school made them weary.

I was the fourth girl in a row, and clothing in those days was made to last forever, so every two years, the teachers not only had another Dalman, but also the recycled clothing. Fortunately for us, we had a very rich cousin in California, an only daughter about the same age as my oldest sister. Every once in a while, my aunt sent boxes of lovely clothing and toys to us, simply because her Thelma got tired of them. When those boxes arrived, it was like Christmas morning. Unpacking brought a series of "aahs" and "oohs" as we impatiently waited for my mom to decide who got what. The oldest had first choice; if something was too small for her, it trickled down to the next. Sooner or later, I inherited some really lovely dresses. I remember a soft, pink dress with a skirt, made of satin and georgette panels. This dress was worn only on Sunday, and when I wore it, I felt like a princess with the world at my command. The illusion was safely hung on a hanger the minute I got home from church.

My mother was a serious student of the Bible, and she considered pride to be the source of all sin. Her example was Satan's fall from heaven. So…wearing lovely things was a problem for her. She considered it a flaunting of herself and felt that being humble was a worthy spiritual goal, not only for herself, but also for her children.

In those days, parents were often very serious, not given to loving exchanges with their children. I have heard from my peers, over and over again, that not once had their parents said they loved them. Emotions were stifled as a sign of weakness. Only once did my mother come close to saying that she loved me. When I was seventeen years old, I had Bronchitis and was running a temperature (this was before antibiotics and often led to pneumonia), and I was sleeping on the sofa near my parents' bedroom. I felt her hand on my forehead and heard her mutter in Dutch, "Sweet little girl", with such tenderness that I thought I might be dying. Recovery brought back the usual sternness, but I suspected then that her terrible fear of God was stronger than her faith. She often talked about her faith, but she was so afraid for herself and for her children, that we would not measure up, and that fear brought on the rules and regimentation that overshadowed God's unconditional love for those who trust Him.

I know very little about my mother's early years. I have often wondered what shaped her into the strong-willed, urgent person she came to be. I do know that she watched two of her little sisters, one a baby and the other a toddler, die of Diptheria, that her father died when she was seven years old and she remembered hearing him in his last hours pleading with God to take care of his family, and that her youngest brother was born two months later. Her mother married again, and her step-father became a stern, remote presence in their home, but he did take care of them. The harsh struggle to just survive was not conducive to a frivolous, carefree lifestyle.

Despite those bleak beginnings, my mother developed a great sense of humor, she spoke of friends, parties, and "outings", of taking the Interurban to Jennison Park on the south shore of Black Lake (later named Lake Macatawa). When her cousins and friends visited in our home, they usually spoke Dutch, laughing and chatting away in the old tongue. It didn't bother me then, but now I wish I could have understood.

My mother was a voracious reader, a habit that carried on to the end of her days. She read every book that we brought home from school, so after the first child went through the school system, she knew what was ahead for the rest of us. I remember coming home from school with a book, and she said, "Oh! I love this book," and dropped whatever she was doing to read to us her favorite story. One day, Harriet brought home "Ben Hur", a new book to Mom. When we left for school that noon, she started to read and was still sitting right there when we got home hours later, weeping at the persecution suffered by early Christians.

My mother had a heart for the many Jewish peddlers that frequented our streets. She would invite them in to view a chart by our front door. She explained to them God's plan of salvation, using the chart to show where God fit into His plan. They always listened respectfully and then left to return again another time and hear it all over again.

When the new Holland Hospital was built up the hill from our home on Cherry Street, we could see when the operating room lights came on at night. Always, my mother would stop everything to pray for whoever was in trouble. My mother prayed a lot; she prayed loud and long for each of her children; she prayed that Roosevelt would see the error of his ways. She belonged to a small group of women friends, who frequently prayed about any meandering from the truth, spotted in our church.

Her strong convictions were enforced in our home, and as the children grew older, they were ready to spread their wings far too early. I married when I was nineteen and rarely attended church after that. I could almost feel my mother's prayers for her wicked daughter ringing in my ears. I found it easy to ignore God, and I had convinced myself that God didn't like me much either.

But God answered my mother's prayers. He gave me a glimpse of His great love for me, and I melted into His arms. I called my mom that Sunday night to tell her that both Gordon and I were back in the fold, and she sobbed, "Praise God, praise God."

Then the battle began. My mother was determined for us to come back to her church, but God had reached us through the ministry of the local Baptist church. We were encouraged there with love and respect, and Pastor Vander Lught never seemed to tire of our immature questions.

That began, for me, a race through the Bible to determine: What is God really like? What is sin and what isn't? Am I, for sure, safely His or just until I do something wrong? What does God require of me? In other words, is salvation really a free gift? I was finding different answers than my mother, which was a real disappointment to her. We had a few intense conversations about our differences, but we were unable to convince her that God's love was unconditional to those who truly put their trust in Him.

During those years after my Dad died, my mother made friends with a blind woman, who also lived alone. Every Sunday night, my mom would visit her by phone and read to her the week's Sunday School papers. That was so typical of my mom. There was no middle ground in her life; she was either kind and compassionate or a formidable force, charging into battle to enforce her perception of truth.

Mom's group of friends continued to uphold the church in prayer, but her relationship with her friends changed after her brother, my uncle Bill, arranged for her to visit each of her children in various places around the country, ending with a stay with him in San Francisco. That was her first and only experience with flying. (Remember, theirs was the generation that traveled by train.) Perhaps she talked too much about the grandeur of things they could never hope to see; maybe they thought she was bragging, whatever…my mother was crushed. That trip was in the summer of 1969.

On the Sunday morning before Thanksgiving, my bother Chuck called from home on Cherry Street, saying that they had arrived on Friday to find Mom recovering from a small surgery on her foot. There was no indication that anything else was wrong, but early Sunday morning, Chuck found her on the bathroom floor. She had escaped her 76-year old body and, in the blink of an eye, had gone from death to life. We spent the next week staying in that old house, so full of memories. It was a good time for all of us.

My mother's body lies next to Dad's in the old cemetery on 16th Street in Holland, Michigan. Her gravestone reads, "I have fought a good fight, I have finished my course, I have kept the faith." I objected to that verse because I thought it made her sound like Carrie Nation, but I was overruled. They said it is truth, and there it stands.

Now, I wonder, does my mother know that the church that she prayed for so faithfully has become a mega church in the ever-growing city of Holland? I think she would be pleased…but then…maybe not.

When I think of my mom, I like to remember hearing her sing as she worked around the house. Her voice was always strong and clear, and I think those hymns were a shelter for her in her struggle for perfection. I share with her a love for the old hymns. Now, sometimes when I stir in the middle of the night and one of those hymns drifts through my mind, I lay claim to it as a bonus from my mother.

Thank you, Mom…. I love you.

Carolyn Dalman Bouman Baker, 07-07

My Father

My father was born on August 10, 1890 into a solid Dutch family. His father, my grandfather, was an architect and builder in the Hope College area in Holland, Michigan. The old Dalman homestead still stands under those tall maple trees on Thirteenth Street.

My dad grew up loving sports and played baseball in his youth. He was a die-hard fan of the Detroit Tigers; that kind of loyalty was part of his character, through thick or thin, that was his team. He also was an amateur photographer, specializing in trains. He was known to hike five miles up tracks just to get pictures of a train wreck.

When my dad was twenty-one years old, he was asked to take pictures at an April Fool's Day party. It was there that he met my mother. She was beautiful, vivacious, a born leader, and full of life. Two years later, they were married.

Then the babies came, every two years or so. Shortly before their fourth child was born, my mother was given a Scofield Bible, which in reading raised some questions in her mind about the practice of baptism in their church. After some discussions with the Domini, she was asked to leave the church. Grandpa Dalman was a founding member of that church and served on the Consistory for years. It was unthinkable that my mom should cause this embarrassment and trouble. Spiritual matters were personal and not to be talked about. She left the church quietly with my dad reluctantly following after. Her in-laws were incensed when she explained her position, and from that time on, we rarely saw any of my dad's family.

I have no recollection of my Grandmother Dalman and only vaguely remember my dad lifting me up to view my grandfather in the casket. My dad continued seeing his brothers and sisters, and after Grandpa died, my dad checked in on his mother every day. This hurt my mother, but Dad's ties to his family were not to be ruptured by theological differences. He stood firm.

When I think of my dad in those years of growing up, my heart smiles. There flashes through my mind so many snapshot pictures of his lighthearted interactions with us. He loved all of us, yet we each claim that we were Papa's pet. We called him "Papa" before we started school, but in school we realized that was "Old Country", and since we were proud Americans, he became "Dad".

I remember Sunday afternoon walks with Dad holding my hand, first one side and then the other so my arm would not get tired. He showed me where he played baseball and where he went to school. He told me about his sister, Kate, who died of Meningitis when she was twelve and dad was a little boy. We usually ended up at the railroad tracks. He was fascinated with trains. We would wait around until a train came by and then wander back home, tired but happy.

I picture, in my mind, my dad coming home from work. The cry would ring out, "Dad's home", and all the little ones would run to greet him with the shout, "My turn for the dinner bucket." That old black container with a domed cover. It usually contained one small treat, a cookie or a piece of candy, or a toy retrieved from a Cracker Jack box. It was such fun for the kids, and he never lost track of whose turn it was.

Storms were another special occasion. My dad would insist that we come down to the dining room, where we cuddled around him on the floor, counting seconds between flashes and crashes, all comfy and safe until the storm passed by. To this day, I enjoy a good storm.

When I started kindergarten, it was required that the student be able to write (cursive) their name, to tie their show laces, and to know the primary colors. On the night before my first day at school, I sat at the dining room table with my dad while I did all three, and he pronounced me ready for school.

In my teenage years, on those bitter cold winter mornings, I would hear at the edge of my sleep, my dad shaking down the ashes in the furnace, and then a little while later, he would call up the stairs, "The Johnny Cake is in the oven. Time to get up", and he was off to work. Away he went, riding his bike the mile and a half to his job as a tool and die maker in a machine shop.

Eventually, we all grew up and then we ushered in the grandchildren for my dad to love. When we all got together for dinners or picnics, you could usually find my dad interacting with the younger ones. He found such joy in them, and I'm so glad some of my children got to know him. Lynda laughingly remembers doing dishes with my dad when she was a child. She was drying and found a dish not quite clean, so she put it back into the dish water. Grandpa looked at her with a twinkle in his eye, and with mock severity, intoned that it was a poor dish wiper that couldn't wipe a dish clean.

My dad never told us that he loved us, but in a million ways the beauty of his love broke through like 24 karat gold. He was a happy man; his gentle humor simmered just below the surface of his life. He was faithful in a difficult marriage and lived with grace and honor to the end. He struggled through those terrible depression years with a large family to feed by working a huge garden with just a shovel and ho, to feed not only his own family, but to also share his bounty with his sisters and brothers and friends along the way. He worked hard at whatever menial odd jobs he could find during those lean years, and never complained. He managed, with the help of his sister, to hang onto our home when foreclosures were crashing all around us. He loved his bike but hated that old Model T, yet he learned to drive it anyway. My dad sacrificed to buy a Bush and Laine piano that he could barely play, so that his children could have music. The ripples from that sacrifice are now being multiplied into his third generation.

My dad, in true Dutch fashion, talked very little about spiritual matters, but long after he was gone and the old house was emptied out, I received as part of my inheritance an old hymn book that was used in our church when I was growing up. Inside the back cover, I found some words from a hymn, copied in my dad's careful handwriting:

He took away my heart of stone
I am the Lord's and His alone
He gives me peace and perfect rest
And holds me closely to His breast.

That's my dad.

Carolyn Baker, 8, 2007

Houses and Storms

When I was four years old, our family moved into a larger home with three bedrooms upstairs and my parents' bedroom downstairs. It was an older home with lots of walk-in closets, an old-fashioned pantry, and a full basement, all on a fifty by one hundred-foot lot.

If a storm blew up during the night, my dad would call up the stairs for all seven of us to come down and sit with him in the dining room. As we got older, we felt that unnecessary, but Dad always wanted all of us there with him. As we sat, cuddled around him on the floor, cozy and comfortable, we knew that no matter how the wind blew or the thunder crashed, we were safe.

I remembered those good times when we had our own family and one of our little ones was terrified at storms. At the first far-off rumble of thunder, our three-year old would come flying into our bedroom, my side of the bed, of course. That night, the storm was putting on a good show. After an especially close flash and window-rattling thunder, a small voice squeaked, "Can I get in the middle?" How we laughed and cuddled him between us! We counted the seconds between the flash and the thunder to help him understand what was happening.

I have often thought how God has a place "in the middle" for me as well. In the storms of life, I can rely on the promises I have stored up in my dining room to quiet me, to give me poise under pressure, and best of all, just to cuddle up with Him and enjoy His presence. He wants for me to do that, just like my Dad.

Once Upon A Time

Before the days when everyone had phones and cars and radios, you could not phone for an appointment if you needed to see a doctor; you would go to the doctor's office as early as you could, get your name on the list, take a seat, and wait your turn. The local family physician took care of almost all the health problems in the community. He delivered the babies, did the surgeries, doled out the prescriptions, and counseled his patients from the cradle to the grave. His importance in the community was right up there next to the preacher, the mayor, the police department, and the undertaker.

In those days, a large percentage of the homes in our community did not have telephones or cars, so if a doctor was needed, you sent for one. House-calls were the norm.

Pneumonia was the dreaded stalker in those days. Most of the houses on our street had front porches. When you passed a house with sheets encasing an area on the porch, you knew someone in that home had Pneumonia. That cold, damp air was their way to aid breathing in the days before oxygen tanks were readily available. In extreme cases of Pneumonia, surgery was used to drain the lungs. Dad was ten years old when he developed Pneumonia, and this operation was a last-ditch stand to save his life. He carried the scars of that surgery on his back for the rest of his life. We never talked about the scars with the children, and I was surprised and amused to learn later that they always thought they were scars from the second World War.

My mother had Pneumonia in the spring, when I was twelve. We watched them take her away on a stretcher, not sure if she would ever come back. For two weeks, she fought through high fevers and dreadful days of struggling to breathe. I remember the day when the strawberries were ripe, and my older sisters and I walked to a farm on the outskirts of Holland to pick strawberries. But first we walked past my mother's room at the hospital, and she waved to us from the window, and we knew then that she would come home again. It is one of those golden days in my memory; God had spared my mother's life.

In the summer of 1945, there was news of a new drug called "Sulfa"; it was to be the miracle drug to wipe out all infections, etc., etc., etc. At about that time, Dad became very ill. We lived in a small apartment in Grand Rapids, Michigan. I went to a phone booth on the corner and called a doctor, and when he came, he found that Dad had Pneumonia, a scary thing for one who had diminished lung capacity to the earlier surgery. He said he would try it in pill form and if it didn't help, there was also another new drug, Penicillin, which is even more potent, but Dad would need to go to the hospital to receive that treatment. Happy to say, the Sulfa worked.

The advances in medicine have been so fast and far-reaching since those long-ago days and all my lifetime. It is hard to grasp. Yesterday, I had a Nuclear Stress Test. I walked in, and three hours later, I walked out. During that time, they had x-rayed every facet of my heart at work. In a few days, I will have a comprehensive report, no doubt with a long list of suggestions on how to manage my health.

Once upon a time, my mother's father died in a Flu epidemic. My mother was seven years old.

Spring of 1929

Private Nurse Miss Leroy

Scarlet Fever (Florence)

Quarantine sign on door.

Dad slept in the basement – so could go to work.

Wood stove in kitchen.

Small bed up on bricks in folks' bedroom for Florence.

Gordy played joke on nurse, pretending to be stuck in the corner space between tub and wall. She fell for it, was angry when we all (7 kids) laughed. Mom scolded and laughed at the same time. I ran a slight fever one day of the quarantine. Spent the day by myself in the corner behind the wood cook stove in kitchen. Miss Skertchy (city health nurse) said I probably had a slight case of Scarlet Fever and would be immune. Harriot, Marion, Florence, and I walked down to the city health department to be examined before being readmitted to school (1st grade). Our house was also fumigated by the city health department before sign could be taken down.

I think mom was pregnant. That's why Florence had to have a private nurse.

HELLO DOLLY

Grandpa Bouman was an avid sportsman with a seasoned knowledge of fishing and hunting. He loved dogs and trained them well. The Bouman family tradition was for the men in the family to go rabbit hunting on Thanksgiving morning while the women prepared the dinner. Dad had many good memories of those years of hunting and fishing with his brothers and his dad, so, of course, when we married, our family included a dog. Our dogs were well behaved; it usually took just one trip around the block for a puppy to learn to "heal" and to "stay". Then came Dolly.

She was such an adorable puppy, a lively ball of fur and full of spunk. We knew it was more than we should pay, but we just couldn't resist. With laughter in our hearts, we walked out the door with our registered Wire-Haired Terrier.

Dad firmly believed any dog could be trained to be man's best friend, and he had lots of experience. Housebreaking was easy. It must have been innate in Dolly's pricy genes because that is all we were able to teach her. She would not come when called or sit or stay or speak or roll over; all those things that other dogs love to do for their proud owners, Dolly treated us with distain. She claimed the wing chair as her own and became part of our family.

At that time, we lived in Steward, Illinois, a small "Bedroom Community" with uptight rules about pets. No dogs were allowed to run free. The town also had a dedicated dogcatcher who loved to enforce the law. $25.00 for every infraction. He loved his job.

One cold, winter night, Dad decided to teach Dolly to "come". After he was sure all the neighbors were asleep in their beds, he bundled up in a heavy wool sweater, put some dog treats in his pocket, fastened a sturdy rope to Dolly's collar, and out they went into the frigid night. I opened the drapes to watch the show. I can still see them under the streetlight, Dad shuffling his feet to keep warm and Dolly dancing and prancing at the end of her tether to break free. Glittering snow crystals were peacefully drifting down on them, indifferent to the coming battle.

Dad called, "Come." Dolly did not budge. Dad pulled her inch by inch, she fighting all the way. Dad patted her, gave her a treat, said "Good dog", and let her go again. Every time, she hit the end of the rope with a choking lurch.

Over and over, Dad repeated the drill, each time encouraging her, saying, "good dog." After a while, the treats ran low. Dad was losing his voice, and his "good dogs" were coming through clenched teeth, but he would not give up. The battle ended after one mighty jerk broke the rope free, and Dolly raced, dragging the rope behind her at a speed that could easily get her to the Mississippi River by morning. When Dad came inside from the cold, he dispiritedly remarked, "A dog who refuses to be trained will soon be dead."

Breakfast was a gloomy affair the next morning. The children didn't expect to see their dog again. Then the phone rang, a neighbor, several blocks to the west, said that our dog was tangled up in her bushes. Would we please come right away before the dogcatcher made his rounds? We were glad to have Dolly safely back come. She settled into her chair like nothing had happened and took a long nap. As the days went by, Dolly became fond of Jack, and we thought there might be hope for her after all.

Several months later, we transferred to Warsaw, Indiana. This was a small town with lots of traffic, not a good place for an independent dog, but we were careful. Nevertheless, in all the confusion of moving, Dolly, waiting for her chance, shot out the door with Jack in chase. Jack's 13-year old legs were no match for that dog, and she was gone. A short time later, a small delivery truck drove up. The driver told us he was very sorry he had run over our dog, and he had taken her to the vet. I was to call the vet and, and his insurance would cover the expenses. The vet said Dolly was badly injured, and I instructed him to put her to sleep. Was that the end of the story? Not yet.

Two weeks later, I received a call from the vet. He had managed to save our dog…would we want to come get her? I told him we did not want the dog, but he was reluctant to put her to sleep because she was such a valuable dog; would we mind if he found a home for her? Permission granted. Still not the end of the story.

The ad was in the Warsaw Times Union for one day: "Registered Wire-Haired Terrier", and we all hoped she would find a good home. Four weeks later, we saw the same ad in the same paper. It had to be our Dolly again, and we all laughed, knowingly. Not too long after that, the ad appeared one more time and then silence…. We never knew for sure what became of Dolly, but with her strength and tenacity, she most likely won the freedom that she struggled so hard to gain, and that would be THE END. Goodbye, Dolly.

Sunday in a Dutch Community

There were about 10,000 people living in Holland when I was growing up. The population was about 85% Dutch adhering to the traditional Dutch covenant theology. They called Sunday the Sabbath and set that day apart to attend church am and pm. There was also a church which held service in Dutch for immigrants, older people, and immigrants in the community on Sunday. After all, the Dutch were a people of strong faith, but their beliefs were heavy in tradition. The rules were rigid:

1. Children did not play outside on Sunday.
2. No restaurants would be open on Sunday.
3. No manual labor.

4. No shopping.

5. No studying on Sunday.

6. A good Dutch housewife would prepare for Sunday simple meals on Saturday to be warmed up for Sunday.

7. No travel, except to services.

8. No Sunday papers, especially the funnies.

9. As circumcision was ordained in the Old Testament, the Dutch tradition

substituted infant baptism, instead firmly believing that was the first step toward salvation, followed by weekly Catechism classes, capped by Confirmation in the early teens.

My mother was given a Scofield Reference Bible and began to study it in earnest the summer before her fourth child was born. She decided that the new baby would not be baptized. Someone from the Consistory came to see her and was dumbfounded that she would go against the traditions of the church. They asked her to leave the church. Dream about trying to reach my mom.

Childhood: My Childhood Hero

Her name was Myrtle Green. I was in the third grade. She was my S.S Teacher. She was beautiful, smelled of perfume, spoke softly, and always kind. I knew for sure that she loved me. I just knew.

She had our class over for a party. Everything was perfect; she served a dessert out of "Better Homes and Gardens": Half banana upright in a pineapple ring with a cherry on top. I didn't know how to eat it, but we watched her – whew. She was a wonderful lady, maybe 25.

What Was the First Movie I Saw?

In the traditions of my solid Dutch family, movies were verboten, but on this Thanksgiving in 1938, the older children, 16 and 21, decided to go for a ride. Somewhere along the way, we decided to see a movie. We drove to Grand Rapids (25 miles) to see "Lady of the Tropics". What an eye-opener. The tropics, so far removed from cold Michigan, the beautiful women, the threatening men.

Favorite movie today: "The Seduction of Doctor Lewis". Opens with a view of the laid-off workers picking up their welfare checks. The plan was to lure a factory to their island, but no doctor on the island and no factory. They advertise and receive an applicant.

American President

Dr. Zhirago

African Queen

Casablanca

Family Secrets

In the years between the first and second World Wars, when I was ten or twelve years old, I remember a cold winter night with all of our big family, cozy around the table, each in our own place. Mealtimes were lively and sometimes noisy, but our manners were important to my mom. No interrupting, be polite, keep your elbows close to your side, say please and thank you, and no one left the table until dismissed.

Suddenly, the pleasant hum of our supper chatter was interrupted by a knock on the back door. My dad went to the door, and we heard muffled greetings from the vestibule. Something important was going on. Dad called my Mom out, and we heard her say, "Thank God"; then there was more muffled talk. But try as hard as we could, it was too hush-hush that we could not hear. We thought it was strange that they stayed out there in the cold. They obviously were friends. Surely, it must be important. Finally, the guests left, and as our parents came into the house, we heard the all too familiar phrase in Dutch, "Niet fer tellen der kintas." (Don't tell the children.)

They did not tell, and we never did find out who those people were, but when we grew older and could keep a secret, we were told the story about a man named John (not his real name).

John was a family relative who served in the military in the first World War. He fought in the trenches in France and was reported, "missing in action". His family mourned him, and the Armistice Day celebrations always brought renewed sadness to them.

The mysterious conversation in the vestibule so long ago was about this man, John. When he was in the thick of battle in France, in all of the confusion, he became separated from his unit. Later, he was rescued by a farmer and was sheltered in his home until after the Armistice. He should have, and normally would have reported back to his unit, but…John had fallen in love with the farmer's daughter. He chose to stay in France. The "missing in action" status was lightyears away from "deserter", and John did not want to shame the family name. At some point in time, John, with a new name, wife, and children, came to the United States as French immigrants. They settled on the East Coast.

John's mother had moved to California, taking most of his siblings with her, but finally he was able to contact someone who could help him connect with the rest of his family. His mother, though getting on in years, was a tough, little old lady and somehow managed to take the train across the country to visit her long-lost son. Her return trip to California included a stop in their hometown to share the good news with a few trusted friends.

Right after Pearl Harbor, the news trickled down by way of the grapevine: John had enlisted in the Navy. The long years of war dragged on. The staggering number of casualties piled up and up and yet, no word from John. Then one day, the dreaded message came; John's ship had gone down… no survivors.

John was safe in the United States. He did not need to go to war. He was too old. He must have lied about his age. But he offered his life a second time, and now the record in his hometown is correct: "Missing in action". We won't mention which war.

This is a true story.

By Ruth Dogger (not my real name)

Wesleyan Church 1936

Pastor's wife, lovely lady, conducted cantatas for Easter. At least I was old enough to be involved in adult activities.

Mrs. Meredith was an accomplished musician and could charm the lowest of us into perfection. My family did a lot of singing together, but this music was a lot more advanced than the simple hymns and choruses. We worked hard; this was a small church, small choir, but the perfection required from each of us was pure joy.

1937

My first love was Art DeFoure. We met at a Youth For Christ meeting. I was 15 and he was 18. I played violin. I had black hair; I wore a red ribbon in my hair. He was smitten. He was tall, blonde, and very serious. Most of our dates were church related or just hanging out at my house, playing games with my family.

He gave me my first Valentine chocolate-covered cherries.

His mother died and I didn't see him for a few weeks; it was over. I was young and frivolous; he was older and serious. Later, he became a minister in the Methodist Church, married and had four kids. He was wounded in the war and died young. My sweet, good-looking, gentle Art.

The Remaking of a Dutch Uncle

Can a man be born when he is old? Can the prison of habits and attitudes, sixty-seven years in the making, be conquered?

"Uncle Bill is coming." The lilt of anticipation caught my interest. Who is Uncle Bill? Must be from the California branch of my mother's family. Later, in a crowded room, I saw this new uncle, a woodsy man, sturdy and upright, face freshly scrubbed with wind and rain. His gentle smile was like a benevolent magnet, drawing a smiling response from even the straightest of faces. A happy man, yet somehow sad.

As I became acquainted with my uncle, the conversation between Jesus and Nicodemus in the third chapter of John's gospel, took on new meaning. "I made a profession of faith in Christ when I was young", uncle Bill said, "but later I drifted away because I was embarrassed around other Christians. So, I avoided visits to Michigan; that's why you don't remember me." He chuckled at his foolishness, then continued, "One Friday, about a year ago, I packed for a weekend of fishing in the mountains with my grandson. Word came of a death in the family in Michigan, but I didn't want to disappoint the boy… then it started to rain."

"Well", he said, "On the spur of the moment, I decided to fly east, go to the funeral and come right back."

"The family housing authority put me at your mother's, and I thought… now I'm in for it; she'll pester me about religion." Then he laughed and said, "I was the one always bringing it up."

The memory of that visit was reflected in the love and tenderness on his face. "She listened quietly to all my objections", he sighed "and only suggested that I should be telling these things to God.

"I couldn't forget it; God had boxed me in with a persistent hunger, and I thought, with jealousy, of her quiet faith. Finally, after days of turmoil, I told God how I felt and only hoped I wasn't ushering in a life of deprivation. God answered by showering me with a knowledge of His presence. My objections melted away, and I basked in the glowing realization of His love."

Then Uncle Bill shared with me about his greedy thirst for the Bible, then quickly added, "I'm retired...have lots of time for reading." He stoutly insisted that the Dutch version of the Psalms is the best, and he read to me from an old Dutch Psalm book of my mother's. For hours, he recounted God's victories in the breaking down of Satan's strongholds and of the battle style in the process. Now I understood the undertone of sorrow, for with his tremendous grasp of God's love came the searing knowledge of God's grief over his waywardness.

The beginning of life in Christ is never an ordinary happening. The totality of my uncle's surrender to God caused him to be an extraordinary example of God's power, set free in a human. His life had not become a trance of ethereal bliss, but rather an enlargement: clean, lively, interested in all aspects of living.

I think back to that week in November, of my mother's death, sudden and irreversible. I do not dwell on the gray, bleak days, but I recall with joy the excitement of my Uncle Bill, full of years, yet miraculously, joyously, made new in Christ.

Can a man be born when he is old? Just ask my Uncle Bill!

Each Day of Life is a Precious Gift from God

When I think of Thanksgiving, I remember the first time I prepared the whole thing from start to finish. My guests were Lil and Hand and their two children. Two weeks ahead, I planned every detail. It was so exciting to do this in our little house; everything turned out well. Now, this was a major event. I rarely had people over. I was scared to death but felt safe with my sister.

1950's Zeeland Michigan

Every fall, our family would go pheasant hunting in Ottawa County, Michigan. Opening day found the farm roads crowded with -out-of-the-area hunters eager to get a shot at the bountiful crop of pheasants in our county.

During the season (three weeks), we would often pack the children in the back seat of the station wagon, and off we'd go, road hunting, all of us scanning and searching for that well-defined head of the ring-necked pheasant. The gun was ready to go. Dusk was the best time. It was a fun family time. My husband was an excellent shot. He was the son of a father who taught his boys good sportsmanship and safety in the sports world.

1955

John Templeton

An attitude of gratitude creates blessing.

Every year for Christmas, we would always get carried away. Always, we determined to stay on budget; always, we charged stuff. So, one year I joined the Christmas club at our bank and didn't tell a soul. On December 1, my check arrived, and I proudly presented it to my husband. Now, did that stop the charging? No way! We just had a wonderful Christmas where wishes did come true.

Dan: 3 years old: rejecting Santa Claus.

December 58, Zeeland

Christmas

Describe the Christmas that has been the most meaningful to you.

Christmas 1958.

Lynda, 15, Dan, 11, Jack, 3, Susie, 5 months.

Gordon and I had become believers on Halloween night that year. Three weeks later, Gordon had an appendectomy: No work for six weeks: No income.

Christmas was just around the corner. Of course, both of our families were in the area and helped us, but what to do for gifts? We bought canning wax and had fun making candles as gifts to our extended families.

God's first big lesson to us was to swallow our pride and accept help.

The Great Blizzard of 1967

When we moved from Holland, Michigan to Sycamore, Illinois in the spring of 1966, housing was scarce, so we rented an old, straight up and down farmhouse that had been renovated. The windows had been replaced with new aluminum castings, nice and neat, but when the wind blew, they whistled. We could pretty well guess how hard the wind was blowing by the pitch of the whistle.

In Michigan, we lived in an area called "The Snow Belt". One winter, I kept a weather journal. We logged 156 inches of snow that year, so you can imagine how amused I was when the schools in Sycamore canceled an event because we had an inch of snow on the ground.

It had been an easy-going winter for us, but we were about to experience our first blizzard on the prairies. I heard warnings on TV, but I was pretty blasé about the whole thing; after all, we were from Michigan. The children were sent home at noon. The bus dropped them off down at the end of the lane, about the distance of a football field from our door. As I watched them struggle against the wind tearing at their clothes with tiny, hard, icy bits of snow, I realized this was no ordinary storm. When they got to the door, I tried to open it, but the wind was so strong, I could barely budge it. Finally, with my pushing and their fingers pulling at the edges of the door, we managed to get it open.

At first, the wind blew laterally, raking the ground clear of every little thing, twigs, stones, or leaves, piling it up at the first obstacle. Then it snowed. The wind forced the tiny pellets of snow through invisible cracks, forming little snow drifts on the windowsills. It was really exciting, and we spent the afternoon going from window to window, watching the snow. Toward evening, a huge drift formed at the back of the house. We tacked up blankets over the back windows to stop the draft and felt very resourceful. So here we were, three miles from town, isolated but knowing that God was watching over us in this sturdy old farmhouse that had weathered many a storm.

My husband called, saying all roads were blocked and he had found shelter at a farm. He was safe and we were safe. We had power, and strangely enough, our phone, which had been a private line, became a party line. It was like going to the bathroom and finding a guest. It was fun chatting on the phone with others in the same situation, and it took the edge off of our aloneness.

The storm howled and the windows keened in an eerie duet all night long while we watched the drama unfolding on Chicago TV. In the morning, I pulled the blanket aside to check on our monster drift; I found bare ground. While we were sleeping, the wind had changed, taking the mountain of snow and depositing it across the front of the house at eye level. It was so beautiful. The wind had created a scrolled top as elegant as a Betty Crocker frosting on a Betty Crocker cake. Who would have dreamed that a storm so wild and ferocious could fashion something so lovely?

Much has been written about the storm of '67. Chicago was shut down for four days. There were 60 deaths attributed to the storm, with no possible way to remove the bodies. Women in labor were transported on toboggans, snowplows, or bulldozers. Northern Illinois was not equipped or funded for a storm like this. Our area, 50 miles west of Chicago, was budgeted for one plowing per snowfall. We were snow-bound for four days. My husband walked in from the main road after two days of zigzagging around the country to find open roads. We sure had a happy reunion.

We all have good memories of the storm. We felt a kinship with the early settlers and the hardships that they endured. Even though we were safe, we were aware of the danger and the awesomeness of nature gone wild. I'm glad that we experienced a real blizzard; it was quite different from the 156 inches of lightly falling snow on the eastern shores of Lake Michigan.

<Untitled, About Driving Cars>

When I drive the busy streets of Tucson, I marvel at the collective skill of the thousands of drivers on our streets, racing to and fro, and for the most part, safely.

I think back years ago to the beginning of America's great romance with automobiles, then often referred to as "machines". I remember our first car, a Ford Model T. It had a few miles on it, but everyone persuaded Dad that he could easily learn to drive. Now, a Model T was not an easy car to master. The first challenge was to get it started. Sometimes the machine needed to be cranked. A special tool, called a crank, was inserted somewhere behind the front bumper and turned quickly to start the motor. If this was done carelessly, the crank could spin around and break an arm just like that!

My dad had zero experience with motors or machines. He was a bike man, but he was game. So, with an experienced friend along to help him, he backed out of the driveway, fiddling with the shift, meshing the gears just so, and after a few jerky lurches, he was on his way. We all watched him go, praying for his safety.

I have been driving for 59 years. I earned my first ticket in 1996 for presuming on the grace of a yellow light. I attended the driver's training class, and it was well worth the cost.

I thank God for the many miles of safe driving, times that I could have been ticketed and times when I was spared in close calls. I am thankful.

WHILE WE WERE KNITTING

By

Carolyn Baker

Knitting is an ancient craft, practiced by men and women, alike. At one time in early England, knitting was an honorable occupation for men. There were elite knitting guilds, whose membership standards were achieved by only the best and fastest knitters. Men are still knitting in Scandinavian countries, as well as in Germany; it is such a soothing, satisfying occupation.

There was a small revival of men knitting in America after the first World War. The Red Cross introduced it to war veterans in recovery, and to this day, the Red Cross method is the standard among U.S. knitters.

I remember watching my grandmother, seated in a straight back chair, knitting wherever my mother was working. I was fascinated as I watched those thin, steel needles fly with the accuracy of a fine-tuned machine; stitch by stitch, loop through loop, she knit sturdy socks for her men-folk while she and my mother chatted away in Dutch.

I have been knitting off and on for the last 70 years, and I think of the history that has evolved while I filled the nooks and crannies of my days with knitting. Rumors of the war were building in Europe and North Africa when I knit my first sweater with two four-ounce skeins of wool. My sister, Harriet, helped me get started and bailed me out when I made mistakes. I was really proud of that sweater.

During the build-up of arms in Germany, I tried a more complicated pattern, using a soft shade of rose; it was lovely, but one day in Latin class, I sat too close to the radiator, and not having a blouse on under my new sweater, it was ruined with indelible perspiration stains, and I was devastated! The troubles in Europe seemed far, far away.

Soon, the rumors of war became thunder, and we were blasted into the second World War. My husband was drafted into the military when I was three months pregnant with our first child. In the long, aching loneliness, I knit for our new baby. Soakers were knit with four-ply wool yarn for diaper protection; no rubber was available for rubber pants. I knit sweaters, booties, and bonnets, and in the knitting were woven all my hopes and dreams for the future. I longed for my husband and for normal family life, and in those lonely hours, I found the primitive act of one stitch after another to be soothing and quieting.

When the war years were over, we entered into the Cold War period of tension with Russia. People build fall-out shelters in case of nuclear attack. It was a scary time, but I kept on knitting; now we had Daniel, who needed mittens on a string and sweaters and caps. When Lynda was in the first grade, I knit a navy, blue gored skirt with matching sweater trimmed in red. It was fun to knit for her; she was the perfect little model.

Hand-knit argyle socks became the "must-have" in those days, and I thought, "Of course I can do that." But I needed help in turning the heel. I went to Steketee's Department store in Grand Rapids, Michigan, where with the purchase of yarn I received all the instruction I needed. With a great feeling of accomplishment, I knit socks, just like my grandmother. I sensed a special kinship with her, and even though we did not share a language, I felt that somewhere she might be saying, "Das Hoet."

The television age arrived in our home in 1950. We watched the first fumbling coverage of a political convention. They caught it all. No one thought to ban the cameras from the back-room wranglings, heated challenges, and side shows. It was raw politics. Nothing was for sure until the last vote from the floor was cast. It was wonderful, all to the drum of Betty Furrness and her Westinghouse commercials and my clicking needles.

When Jack was born, my husband bought a rocking chair for our new baby. That chair also became my knitting chair. There, I worked into my stitches the happenings of a world streaking by. General MacArthur was ousted from the South Pacific by President Truman. What an uproar! We watched our first Olympics in black and white, while I knit a sweater with a caramel design on a cream background. I knit through "Gun Smoke", and "All in the Family", and "You Asked for It", and football games beyond number. In that same rocking chair, we rocked our second daughter, Susan, and three years later, our third son, Sam.

One day, in November, as I returned home from purchasing more yarn, the phone was ringing; it was Helen Hubble with the news about President Kennedy having been shot. That moment is like a snapshot firmly fixed in my memory. There I stood, reaching to catch the phone, struggling with packages, baby in arms, bulky, winter clothes, snowy boots; life came to a sudden halt. Soon, it was announced: President Kennedy had died. Terrible sadness shrouded the whole country as we watched the cortege, the pageantry, the long procession under the leafless trees, the traditional horse without a rider, boots backward in the stirrups, the somber slow beat of the drum; the burial and the events that followed came live to us in our Living Room. We were numb. I put down my knitting and we watched on in silence, heavy with sadness.

We looked forward to the next presidential conventions, but they were not the fun of the first coverage on TV. The cameras were restricted, and the events were orchestrated to show politicians at their Sunday best. Too bad!

Lynda went off to college when Sam was a year old. She wanted me to knit an Irish sweater for school. The pattern was too complicated to do with three little ones underfoot, so for a couple of hours every day, I holed up in my bedroom, knitting like crazy while Lynda watched the children. The sweater was finished just in time for her first venture into the big world away from home.

Eventually, Lynda finished college, married her Bill, and they set off as missionaries to Iceland. ICELAND! I could see it in my mind. A land of Eskimos, snowshoes, and sub-zero temperatures; but I was wrong. Iceland, brushed by the Gulf Stream, has summers like San Francisco and about the same amount of snow as Northern Michigan. Because of the Danish influence in their country, Iceland has become a highly developed society with 100% literacy and rich beyond all expectations in arts and crafts. My first package from Lynda contained knitting patterns and wool straight off the sheep on the volcanic mountains of Iceland.

When my husband's company transferred us to Northern Illinois, Dan stayed in Michigan to finish college. The political conventions were in Chicago that year; the big issue was the Viet Nam War. Turmoil was rampant on college campuses. With heavy hearts, we saw our son with diploma in hand, leave for Canada. He went to a place we did not know, and into my knitting I stitched prayers for his safety and a heart yearning for the day we would see him again.

At about that time that I started watching a knitting program on TV, which was taught by Elizabeth Zimmerman. Knitting and rocking, she taught how to knit a pullover by knitting round and round with no seams and then horrors! She showed us how to cut the sweater down the front to make a cardigan. I did it! With that wonderful Icelandic yarn and the distinctive Icelandic patterns, I knit more sweaters than I could count.

On one of our many trips to Canada, Dan and I shopped for just the right yarn for a Canadian sweater. It was fun to tackle the project on our way back to

Indiana. Knitting away those long miles over the mountains and the prairies, I knit and imagined how nice he would look in his new grey sweater. Would his friends mention how nice he looked? Would he tell them that his mother made it? Probably not.

One summer, while visiting my sister, Marian, in Michigan, I watched her knitting a lace afghan. I thought maybe I could do that. I copied the pattern from a tattered piece of paper that had been given to her by a friend. It did not have a name, and the pattern was hard to decipher, but Marian helped me get started, and I was back to knitting again. It was a new challenge, complicated, requiring a careful count of stitches and concentration. There were times when I wasn't sure I could do it, but after many errors, unraveling and re-knitting, it was finally finished. Now, if given enough warning, it has become my favorite wedding gift.

My grandmother learned to knit in the late eighteen-hundreds. Over the years, while we were knitting, our world has changed. The knitting traditions have carried on from my grandmother, Henrietta Dykstra, to my mother, Tillie Dalman, to me, Carolyn Baker, to my daughters, Lynda Bergin and Susan Kellner, and to their daughters, Nina, Natalie, Abi, and Gillian.

It was pleasant this past summer to watch my granddaughters knitting while they chatted together, and I thought how lovely it is that they are finding the same deep soul satisfaction that I have known to be useful in knitting attractive items for those that we love.

CHAPTER TWO:

Dated Writing Class Assignments and Journaling, 2001–2009

9/11

<*Someone*> has perfected the plan to hijack planes, to fly them, loaded, into crowded buildings. Dear Father, comfort the wives and husbands and children left behind. Open their hearts and minds to Your Word. I weep for them in their grief. I pray also for this country, for President Bush, for those who are working in the disaster areas. Give them strength and skill for the awesome task ahead.

Psalm 103: 15-17

As for man, his days are like grass;

as a flower of the field, so he flourishes.

For the wind blows over it, and it is gone,

and its place remembers it no more.

But the mercy of the Lord is from everlasting to everlasting in those who fear Him.

The brevity of Life is an expression of grace for those who hope in Jesus Christ. – Walter Henrichsen.

September 18, 01

Psalm 77, vs. 1-8: Complaining to God in despair – have you forgotten me?

vs. 10: And I said, "This is my anguish, but I will remember the years of the right hand of the most high God." I will remember how He sought me out, how he made me hungry for Him. How he crafted circumstances, people, and my desperate needs to prepare me, to nullify my clever reasonings, to bring me to complete dissatisfaction with myself and longing for peace with Him. I remember how God opened my eyes that Fall afternoon (1958), when I went to His Word and dared Him to show me that I should do something so far out as "GET SAVED". I wanted God but was scared to death of the "church" and all its trappings, the homogenized minds, the social restrictions, the politics, conforming the members to an indistinct similarity. My mind cried, "God made me…ME…not a copy of thee!" But God said in Matthew 18, "Come to me just as Jack and Susie come to you. I want to love you just the way you love them. I want to take care of you, enjoy you, and for you to enjoy me. I want to teach you my ways, share with you my secrets." And I felt as though God's very arms were around me, flooding me with his Love. In verse 8 of Matthew 18, He also said, "I know what goes on in the church, but don't worry about it. I will take care of it." And I cuddled close to Him and didn't know that I had gotten "SAVED".

Yes, Lord, I remember those early days, how you had this wonderful little church with a caring pastor, always ready to explore my immature questions, helpful but dictatorial, kind and gentle. I remember, Lord, how you brought a friend into my life, who was in love with your Word, how she shared her enthusiasm with me and encouraged me, by example, to memorize the scriptures. "And I ate your words in memorization and your words became unto me the joy and rejoicing of my heart." – Jeremiah 15:16. "Your way is in the sanctuary of your word! Who is so great as our God?" – Psalm 77:13.

You changed me from a frightened, young mother and wife to a trusting, "full of years" woman. Please continue to guide my ways. Help me to be quiet, that I may hear Your voice, and some of the goodness that You have given to me will be shared with those You have put into my life. And now as I leave the horrors of last week in Your hands, I deliberately remember who You are and that You are my Father. I need nobody else, for "Who is so great as our God?" – Psalm 77:13.

Thoughts on forgiveness:

Ephesians 4:32: Be kind and compassionate to one another, forgiving each other, just as in Christ, God forgave you.

Psalm 32:5: Then I acknowledged my sin to you and did not cover up my iniquity. I said, "I will confess my transgressions to the Lord." And you forgave the guilt of my sin.

Luke 23:34: Jesus said, "Father forgive them, for they do not know what they are doing."

John 20:22, 23: "Receive the Holy Spirit (Ephesians 1:13B Having believed, you were marked in Him with a seal, the promised Holy Spirit). John 22, vs. 23: "If you forgive anyone his sins, they are forgiven; if you do not forgive them, they are not forgiven."

November 29, 2001

II Corinthians 4:7-18

After listing the pressure points in my life right now, I needed to write.

Dear, Lord Jesus,

Well, here I am, Lord; 79 years old, older than I ever expected to be, with a passion and a purpose for being here. Forgive me for even mentioning the side effects of aging. When I view my life through Your eyes, I feel like a child crying because the ice cream is gone. Help me to see with Your eyes, to seek out Your mind, that as I lose physical strengths, I may gain spiritual acuity, to reflect You in all things.

Thank you.

I love you.

Good night.

August 5, 2005

Jennifer Beauchamy's Class

What fun things do you want people to know about you?

1. I'm a recovering practical joker.
2. I love to hear people laugh.
3. I appreciate a good joke.

Finish these sentences.

1. **When I think of trees**, I remember my toddler years and the cotton-woods in the side yard. What were they saying as they whispered in the night? Were they telling secrets? Were they saying, "Don't touch me" or "Come closer?" Whatever; I'm sure it was nice.

2. **I hit him** with a flip of my hand, coy and flirty. How else would a nice girl respond? Later, he wrote, (Sunday night in church) "Sweetness was the nature, snappy was the creed, but the first time I attempted, I found her hand had speed."

3. **The clouds were white** and billowy as we drove endless miles across the Midwest, three kids in the back of a Volkswagen. We pretended they were castles or ski runs or high ocean waves. We took turns telling stories about what we imagined in the sky.

8-05

Nice Fresh Celery, Five Cents a Bunch

It was early spring in Holland, Michigan, 1932. The country was in the depths of the Great Depression. My dad had lost his job, and there were nine mouths to feed in our home. My dad arranged with a local market to pick up, with a coaster wagon, two big boxes of celery from the muck farms nearby.

Every Saturday, my sister and I, ages ten and twelve, would set out to sell the celery door to door. Our mantra was, "Nice, fresh celery, five cents a bunch." All the money was turned in to our dad. Facts of life.

We trudged all morning in no hurry, talking, spotting the first robins of spring. Early entrepreneurs we were not. It was almost noon and we had two bunches of celery left and a storm was brewing. As we passed a block of shops, we found a small coin purse on the sidewalk. It contained 35 cents. In those days, a hamburger sold two pounds for a quarter and coffee 19 cents a pound. It would also buy a Yo-Yo, the craze that year. My parents did not have money for toys. Facts of life.

We quickly decided to sell the celery and go shopping for a Yo-Yo. Prices ranged from ten cents to maybe 50 cents for a real fancy one. Just as we ran up the steps of the next house, the storm broke. Before we could knock on the door, it flew open and an old lady chided us for being out in the storm and asked us to wait until it blew over. She was distraught; she had just returned from the market and couldn't find her coin purse.

Well! We had just come off of a revival meeting in our church, had gone to the alter again and again, confessed our sins again, and we promised God we would never sin again. I looked at my sister and we nodded "good-bye" to the Yo-Yos. The lady was so grateful that she fixed us lunch and chatted with us like we were long-lost friends. And then, as we were leaving, she slipped us a bright, shiny dime, enough for one "bottom-of-the-line" Yo-Yo. We headed for home, a couple of lighthearted kids. Life was good.

C.R. Baker

09-28 ‹2005?›

Christmas When The Money Stopped

My big sister, Marian, was the champion in those lean depression years. Early in the fall, she would start gathering ideas and materials we could make for Christmas. She brought out the lovely foil, saved from last year's Christmas cards to be transformed into vases, scraps of cloth, never new but usable, for pin cushions and potholders and stuffed dolls. We created works of "art" from calendar pictures and crayon renderings, which Marian framed, rough but hangable.

For a while, my mother considered Christmas trees pagan. Marian created a fireplace out of boxes and covered it with brick-patterned crepe paper. Small logs, from the woods across the field, with red tissue paper crunched between looked almost real with our eyes all squinty and dreaming. We made swags of paper chains, all read and green, and somehow the pile of gifts grew. After a while, my mother relented on the Christmas tree issue, and it was Marian who scouted for the trees tossed out when vacation started at school. Marian fashioned a base of scrap wood to keep it upright. She also started the tradition in our family of feeding the birds, no fancy bird food, just homemade breadcrumbs. We were always entertained as we tried to identify them all. Several kinds of sparrows, juncos, cardinals, chickadees, and if the winter was especially harsh, the evening grosbeaks, brilliant, all yellow, black, and white, came down from the North. My children called them the "painted birds".

My heart still warms when I think of the giving of handmade gifts and the love that inspired them, the laughter as my mother opened yet another package of potholders, the reading of the Christmas story, and the singing of carols. We were a sometimes-scrappy family, but the joy of the season eclipsed all the hardships, and our hearts were thankful.

C.R. Baker

09-30-05

"Crash" DVD

I saw, rather I heard, a rasping noise outside my kitchen window. The noise persisted; finally, I put my work aside and investigated. Then I saw a lower branch in the tree by my kitchen window, a large bird, speckled breast, a hawk's bill opening and closing his mouth at intervals, sounding like he had severe laryngitis. Its tail was not tapered, but like it had been squared. With that much to go on, I searched my old, faithful birding book and decided it was a cooper's hawk. I've never been that close to a cooper's hawk before.

10-07-05

When I think of Sunday afternoons in the summer, I remember, when I was six or seven years old, my dad asked who would like to go for a walk. I was the only one who volunteered, so off we went, just the two of us. Every block or so, he would change sides so my arm wouldn't get tired. He told me about the tradition of men walking on the street side when being out for a walk with a lady, to protect her from the traffic in the streets.

Walking with my dad always ended up at the railroad tracks. This particular Sunday, we picked wild strawberries alongside the tracks, talking some but just enjoying the afternoon. I knew we would putter around there until a train came by. My dad was fascinated with trains. He was an amateur photographer, complete with a tripod camera and a black cloth to throw over his head. He loved to photograph trains and was known to hike five miles up the track to get pictures of a train wreck.

Eventually, the train came and didn't slow up much for our little town.

Then, slowly, we made our way back home again, passing houses with good Dutch people, rocking away on their front porches, exchanging greetings. Everyone liked my sweet, gentle dad. I get pleasantly drowsy just thinking about those days, like a really good dream that somehow flew away.

10-21-05

First Day of School as a Child

I was four years old, almost five. I walked to school with my sisters. I was a little shy but accustomed to being with a group. My sisters were in the 2nd, 4th, and 6th grades. Kindergarten required you to write your first name, tie your own shoelaces, and know the colors. The night before, I sat in the dining room and wrote my name, cursive, with my dad. He pronounced me ready.

10-21-05

The Romance of Music

What a joyful thing, God giving us music. He must have designed the harmonies and tempos in heaven and then instilled into our minds and hearts, the desire to go beyond the spoken word to bring praise to Him with music.

As far back as I can remember, I have enjoyed music. When we moved to the big house on Cherry Street, our old Victrola was moved down to the basement. I remember cranking it up over and over again to listen to a certain piece of music sung on an ancient record by a quartet of mixed voices. It was so grand; like four different voices singing together but each on their own flying trapeze. They would connect, disconnect, melody, and counter-melody. Different tempo patterns, complicated, yet always perfectly synchronized, and in the end, they all came together, beautiful notes hugging each other in one grand chord. I was hooked.

We got our first piano shortly after that. It was a Bush and Lane, manufactured in our town. It was a big thing with elephant legs, elaborately carved. My oldest sister began playing very soon and went on to become a good pianist. Our schools at that time gave us a solid foundation in music. We were taught how to read music, so it wasn't much of a leap from there to hymn books and then to the classics.

When I entered junior high, the school offered classes on different musical instruments. We had an old violin at our house, which was fixed up at Myer's

Music House for $4.52. That introduced several wonderful years for me. I played in the senior orchestra during high school and loved it. My sister and I had many wonderful hours working together, I on the violin and she on the piano, but life moved on. My sister went off to college and then married, and it was like a lost love that had no hope of a future.

Our family, being a good Dutch family, read the Bible and had prayer after each meal. But, in the evening, my dad would read a Bible story book to us at the table. We loved it; we would ask, "Please one more." Then after that, instead of praying, we would sing a hymn or a chorus or two. It was there that I learned to sing harmony. We all enjoyed it so much. The wonderful words and music in those hymns have stuck with me all the days of my life. Still, in the night, I wake up with those melodies and words in my mind. In the 15 years that we were away from the church, my husband and I often sang hymns as we traveled in the car. They were like God's tether, letting us go our own way but always the gospel was there. "What can wash away our sins? Nothing but the blood of Jesus. What can make me whole again? Nothing but the blood of Jesus." God is faithful.

In October of 1958, our oldest daughter attended a Youth For Christ meeting and received Christ as her savior. Soon she had her friends praying for her wicked parents, and God answered her prayers. We attended a Baptist church in Zeeland, Michigan. Once again, we were involved in church music. I no longer had a violin, but God granted me the opportunity to once again sing in a ladies trio and choir. What a blessing to my soul to be restored to singing again of God's wonderful love. Somewhere in the Old Testament, God speaks of restoring the wasted years. He has done that over and over. Later, I picked up a violin at an auction and started over from scratch; really painful. I have not attained the ability I once enjoyed, but I am still working at it and am enjoying every minute of it.

After my husband died in June 1996, God ministered to me in the long evenings; I, plinking away on the piano and God bringing comfort to my soul through the wonderful poetry found in the hymn books and the contemporary song of today.

Tim and Martena Baker were friends of ours. We often visited together. Martena died in February the same year that Gordon died in June. I had no interest in another marriage. One day, I was at a missionary meeting at Tim's house. Tim asked me to stay and play the piano for him as he sang. I thought, "He will only ask me that once. Piano is not my forte." But not so. A few months later, we married. Oh my, could that man sing!! I was attracted to Tim because he reminded me so much of my dad: quiet, gentle, funny in a sneaky sort of way, and best of all, he really loved Jesus. We had four wonderful years together.

10-28-05

My best memory of camp is when we decided to chuck everything and head out to Ottawa Beach, Holland Michigan, my old stomping grounds. When I was in high school, many of my friends spent the first week of summer camping. But my mom wouldn't let me, so those days in June always made me feel deprived. So, Gordon and I threw a bunch of things in the car and headed out 12.5 miles away.

We pitched our tent late in the afternoon and soon realized we were in the middle of a mob of teenagers ready to party. The tradition had survived; it was fun to be a spectator.

10-28-05

Road Trip: First Trip to Vancouver

Dan had left for Canada in 1971. We had not seen him for five years. In August 1976, we decided to make the long trek in a new Dodge Aspen Station Wagon.

We had ten days. We arranged mattresses in the back, packed some food, and set out from Warsaw. I had never been west of Kansas City. I had read every Zane Grey ever written, and now we were at last going to see the West. We stayed at motels on alternate nights, ate one big meal in a restaurant per day, and snacked every mile, bringing us closer to our first son. It was a wonderful trip. The C.B. radio kept us entertained, listening to other travelers talking about the history of the places we passed. We left Warsaw on Friday and arrived in Vancouver Monday night. What a reunion.

1-13 ‹2006?›

One special thing I did this Christmas was find time at my daughter's house to just enjoy people, the little bodies flying around, the ear-splitting screeches, just one decibel short of rock music, the joy of watching a toddler explore his universe, all conversations shouted above the joyful clatter. I didn't fix a simple meal or clean anything up. Age has its perks. That was a first.

"It's easy to be brave from a safe distance."

1983

With no bookkeeping experience, I accepted the position of Office Manager for "Win-Some Women" in Winona Lake, Indiana. I received all the materials and instructions from the previous manager, who was also a private secretary to the president of a college. I was overwhelmed; so much of the work was redundant, sending unnecessary correspondence, poor accounting, etc., etc.

When the reservations started pouring in for the next retreat, I didn't have a clue as to how I would keep track of four different plans and three different housing places. I needed to chuck everything I'd been told and simplify to something I could visualize.

02-04-2006

One of my favorite toys was roller skates. It granted me the freedom of the streets. Our part of town had gentle hills, and I can still feel the exhilaration of flying down the hill, coasting to a stop, and then puffing up the hill to do it all again. Spring was so long in coming to Holland, Michigan, so when the weather started warming up, we appreciated it doubly. We had the run of the town and roller skates was my favorite way of seeing it all.

Worn-out wheels, lost skate keys, and hot weather usually brought it to an end.

All too soon summer was over, and the cooler weather, along with the school schedules, ended the long days of carefree play.

I liked school, and somehow in the early grades, we learned our lessons with very little homework. That left us with time at home for family fun. The games that we played at home were the classics, like Checkers, Chinese Checkers, Pick Up Sticks, and some early versions of Scrabble. My dad liked to play Caroms with the boys, and often, we would clear off the dining room table to play Ping Pong. It was by no means a standard set-up, but we had great fun with lots of noise and banter.

That is what it was like when I was growing up. When I entered the teen years, I spent more and more time reading or knitting. Junior high and high school required much more homework, and I also spent a fair amount of time practicing the violin. Life was full and good. I do not remember ever being bored.

Years later, I heard for the first time, a ten-year old whine, "I'm bored." I looked at her in astonishment, thinking, is she retarded? There are a million books she hasn't read, endless puzzles to be solved, games to play, stories to write, pictures to draw, music to hear and songs to sing, flowers to plant, birds to identify, stars to name, and mountains to climb. Have we deadened her senses by smothering her with things, superfluous stuff? I hope not, I really do hope not.

C.R. Baker

02-10-2006

<My Dad's Garden, Rough Draft>

When I picture a garden, I think of my dad, quite hardworking, with a gift for raising the best garden in the world. He would ride his bike to work in the morning, go from there to a rich plot of ground. In the afternoon, he would work the garden with love and skill. He would come riding in during the evening, loaded with fresh veggies, having stopped on the way home to share with his sister and some other friends along the way. It was his life-long hobby. He spaded over the rich river muck on his plot by hand, and his gentle soul was nourished, as well as all those who received from his bounty.

Class Quickie 02-10-2006
My Dad's Garden

When I picture a garden, I think of my Dad, gentle, hardworking, with a gift for raising the best garden in the world.

He rode his bike to work in the morning and then go from there in the afternoon to a plot of ground at the North end of College Avenue. There, he worked his garden from early spring until late fall, planting and harvesting every kind of vegetable imaginable. He would come home at dusk, loaded with fresh produce, having stopped along the way to share with his sister and other friends.

Gardening was my Dad's lifelong hobby. He took pleasure in every phase of the work, from spading over the rich river muck on his plot of ground to harvesting and sharing his rewards with others.

1961: Oral Copy: 02-24-2006
My Sister Harriet

My sister, Harriet, was the oldest daughter in a family of twelve. Our older brother was quick, smart, and full of fun and noise, but Harriet was a quiet, sweet child, almost lost in her brother's shadow. My parents thought that she was "slow". Her health was fragile, and she tired easily; Harriet was "the tortoise" to her brother, "the hare". Steadily and quietly, she plodded through her school years.

When she was 12 years old, my parents bought a piano, and that was the turning point in Harriet's life. She taught herself to play out of the hymn book; then when I started playing the violin and brought home the classical music that I played in the high school orchestra, she took to it like a duck to water. Together, we explored the wealth of music written for piano and violin. We spent many happy hours playing together, laughing at our mistakes, and pushing on. She would not settle for second best. We kept trying until we got it write. It was great, satisfying fun.

There was a lot of work to be done in our large family. We all had our chores, but Harriet saw to it that I had time to practice. She was such an encouragement to me; she was not just my sister, but my friend and mentor.

When my mother's health failed, Harriet was taken out of high school to help at home. She never complained. It was accepted by all of us that we work together for the good of the family.

When Harriet was 20, my parents let her return to school, while the younger sisters took their turns at staying home. When she graduated, now 22 years old, she went to work at Heinz Pickle Factory, a terrible place to work. (That place has inspired a lot of people to pursue higher education.) My mom was sure that she would not last the first day. But she did. She earned enough to see her through one year at Western Michigan Teacher's College.

She lived with a small family, working for her room and board. Another summer at Heinz and a second year of college gave her a teacher's certificate. Her first job was in a two-room school, out in the country. As part of her salary, a school board member provided lodging and meals with his family.

She taught there until she married a minister, and they moved away. We saw each other every few weeks. My home was always their first stop when they came to town. I missed her, but we were both now having children, and our ways had separated. I was no longer playing the violin, and I also had stopped going to church.

She never scolded me about my life; she just quietly loved me. Harriet always seemed to bring out the best in me, even in those bad years. With her, I felt confident, loved, and hopeful. She cared deeply for me, but her faith rested in God and not in her ability to persuade me. I envied her faith, but I didn't think it was possible for me to ever live the life that she lived.

Eventually, God answered her prayers, broke down my barriers, and welcomed me back into his fold.

I wrote her a letter, telling her about my new life. She shot a letter back to me, praising God and encouraging me but did not ask, "What church", a major question at that time. It didn't matter to her. God was in charge. A few weeks later, she sent me a beautiful Bible, my true love letter from God and from my sister.

Three years later, Harriet had a hysterectomy and developed a blood clot, which took her life.

Often in the years since then, I have had these impulses to talk to Harriet, a longing to share with her about Susie, who has become a professional accompanist on the piano. Or I want to tell her that I am again playing the violin and about the fun that Nancy and I have murdering Mozart. I would like her to know that the encouragement that she gave me has been passed on to my children, and now to their children. Like a pebble thrown into a pond, the ripples of encouragement keep moving out, and I wonder; does she know?

We are told that when we sing praises to God, all the hosts in heaven join our worship. I would like to think that Harriet is a part of that. Of one thing I am sure, if I could hear her now, she would whisper, "You're doing great; keep it up."

02-24-2006

When I think of the rodeo, I remember all the Zane Grey novels I devoured as a child. The Wild, Wild West was a far country from Holland, Michigan, but in my dreams, I lived it.

When we made our first cross-country trip to Vancouver, British Columbia, we had a CB radio in the car. As we passed through the West, someone on the CB gave us the story of Custer's Last Stand. It was on that hill that this happened. It was over there. I felt like I was living it in person.

03-24-2006

This week, when I saw the snow on the mountains, I remembered the winters in Michigan. We lived in an area with gentle hills, and we spent lots of time sledding and skiing. We made fox and geese patterns and snow forts, fortified with lots of snowballs for ammo. We didn't have snow suits in my day, but we layered on extra clothing. And when we were soaked through, we would come in and hang the clothes to dry. Then, as soon as they were dry, we would go out and do it all over again.

06-09-2006

My mom could rule the world, but my dad took care of the money. Every week, he would get out his box of envelopes on pay day, carefully marked, and divide his paycheck: two dollars here, five dollars there. Once in the envelopes, it never was withdrawn for any other purpose than stated on the envelope. I never heard any agreements or disagreements about money. I know my mom had cash for groceries and the frequent peddlers, but in our home, considering the size of our family and the meager years, I never heard an argument about money. Dad did a good job.

06-16-2006

Quickies

My favorite past-time as a child was reading. With so many siblings, it was my escape to other worlds. There was a bookcase next to a recliner in one corner of the dining room. The space in the corner was my hideaway. My mother hid her mending in a box back there, and it was my throne. As soon as I was old enough (3rd grade) to walk alone to the library, my corner was always there for me with the latest book.

When my parents died, we could name what we wanted out of the house. All I wanted was the bookcase, crafted by my paternal grandfather. The next trip to Canada, we took it to Dan, who is also an excellent cabinet maker, to be sure the bookcase stayed in the family.

Changes: 17 years in Warsaw, 15 years with Win-Some Women (closer than family), leaving behind our little house, with large windows showing trees, birds, playful squirrels, my pleasure in watching the wildlife in the changing seasons.

The furniture was left; we were all packed. And where were we going? To the desert – visions of sitting on a sand pile in the middle of nowhere.

God had plans for us beyond my wildest dreams. The modular home we had purchased in Tucson needed much help.

07-28-2006

Quickies

This week, I saw new opportunities in friendships at F.H.E. My prayer is that I may be of help and encouragement. I'm more keenly aware of the brevity of our lives, due to the sudden loss of Pauline Brooks with a massive stroke. And this new friend – God help me.

Fourth of July at Far Horizon's East.

A large percent of the men living at F.H.E. served in World War II. I had forgotten what old-fashioned patriotism was like until I watched this group put together a 4th of July celebration. First order of the day was gathering around the flagpole as the flag was raised and the salute. Then the parade, home-made floats, decorated cars, and the men, serious and reverent, marching in their uniforms, pride in every step.

This was followed by a breakfast of sausage and egg sandwiches, fruit, and coffee.

A program followed with a reading about the development of our flag and the history of its changes, read by a grown man who could hardly keep his emotions under control.

10-4 <2006?>

Banana Bread

When I eat, I always remember our rare trips to Getz Farm. In Lake Michigan, my dad drove the Model T, the back two deep in kids, the youngest on my mom's lap. We would pack a lunch and head out to this fabulous place on the lake. My first memories of a zoo – we needed to go back out to the car to eat – not allowed inside the zoo area. I close my eyes and can see us gathered around, eating that wonderful banana bread. It is the same recipe I use to this day!

10-06-2006

This year, I want to be more disciplined with my time to determine what needs to be done and then stay focused. It's like I'm fighting a tide that is carrying my hours away with very little to show for it. I need to prioritize and not imitate Snoopy, who lays on top of his doghouse saying, "LEARN FROM THE PAST, PLAN FOR THE FUTURE – REST THIS AFTERNOON."

10-06-2006

Children At Play

I was raised in the middle of a large family with sisters near my age, so we had lots of fun playing together. I had school friends, but my sisters were my real friends.

My brothers did "boy things", like digging holes, making forts, climbing trees, and catching wild things (which my mother made them return to the wild). They played marbles and flew hand-made kites. They damned up the creek across the street, and as the water piled up, they worked feverishly to keep it from breaking, and when it did, it was quite a show; that is what my brothers did for fun.

We all played out of doors a lot in good weather. Our games were primitive with few props. The girls played Hop-Scotch, and Skip-Rope. We challenged each other to see who could jump the furthest or highest. We would take turns sitting, blind-folded, in the coaster wagon while we were taken for a ride, and then we had to guess where we were.

We often walked to the Longfellow School playgrounds to play on the swings, teeter-totters, monkey bars, and giant strides. We played Jacks, scraping our knuckles across the cement, trying to grab the jacks before the ball bounced again.

We had supervised play for part of the summer, and it was there, sitting under the tall oak trees that I learned the basics of embroidery, and I remember coming home with a swatch of cloth to show my mother my first attempts at backstitching and daisy petals. She was impressed.

Summer evenings often would find us with all the other kids in the neighborhood playing Hide-and-Go-Seek or variations of that game. Goal was under the streetlight on the corner. We would play hard all evening while the parents sat on their front porches watching the fun. When the streetlights came on, my dad would call us home with his own distinctive whistle. I can still recall the sound of that whistle in my mind. It was like the call of a Killdeer, only louder. I never, not even once, heard my dad yell at us. His special whistle was enough.

One big adventure was to drive to Zeeland, five miles to the East. Dad decided to take a less traveled route, but it had one problem: Approaching Zeeland from the South presented a steep, short hill. Before we started up the hill, Dad told us that if the car stalled, we were to get out quickly on the right-hand side. I remember the rigid tension and the united sighs of relief as we made it to the top.

We had a lighthearted drive back to Holland, stopping at a gas station that was celebrating their grand opening with candy bars for adults and balloons for children. When Dad paid his bill, they asked how many children, and my dad said, "7." They said, "No way" and came out to check. Sure enough, one on mom's lap in the front and six of us double-deckered in the back seat.

I was eight years old that fall. The next year was the beginning of the great depression, and eventually the Model T was traded to our milk man to cover our milk bill.

In 1948, Dad purchased a 1934 Ford. I was 16 that year, and we learned to drive together. It gives me pleasure to remember that was the beginning; by the end of the summer, he was managing to drive quite well, but he always seemed to view the car as an enemy to be conquered.

Labor Day marked the end of Summer. School always started the next day. For a treat, it was decided that we would all go for a ride in the "Model T".

08-24-2006

If somebody wanted to buy a gift for your collection, what would you like?

A ceramic Pileated Woodpecker in memory of seeing that beautiful, statuesque bird out of Dan's kitchen window, deep in the woods of British Columbia. It would be an impressive addition to my bird collection of three.

My daughter, Susie, and her husband are avid sailors, so the décor in their home is nautical. They collect lighthouses and will travel miles out of the way to visit them in person. They have visited many of the lighthouses in their collection. Mark is a composer and has written a piece called "Barque Sofraic" about a small sailboat in a storm.

11-06

My Recipe Box

I have a very old recipe box, stuffed with memories: the events, the happy occasions, the important happenings all flood my mind and the people who have contributed are right there, life-size, as I picture the setting, the smells, the laughter, the anticipation, and sometimes up-tight presentation. Of course, I had my times of failure, of last-minute substituting the alternatives in a recipe, but I learned to laugh, knowing that sooner or later, mistakes happen in every kitchen.

My earliest memory of food was eating dinner (noon) the day we moved to Cherry Street. The table wasn't set up, so we stood around eating with plates on whatever we could find. The hamburger tasted heavenly. The taste buds of a four-year old were at their best.

There flashes through my mind the many scenes of my mother, who loved to cook but rarely had all the necessary ingredients but was happy in the endeavor. The aroma of Apple John baking in the oven (a quart jar of apple sauce, topped with baking powder biscuits and a generous sprinkling of cinnamon sugar) is one of our favorites. Later, with my own family, I made this, and the response was, "What is this?"

My dad liked to bake as well. He left for work at 6:30 in the morning, and often on those cold, winter mornings, he would call up the stairs on his way out the door, "The Johnny Cake is in the oven." I can close my eyes and still see my dad on a Sunday morning at the kitchen sink, happy as can be, preparing and assembling a seven-layer dinner. He would put it into the pressure cooker, bring it up to steam, then shut it off. It would be ready for us when we came home from church.

During the depths of the depression, another baby was due, so my mom taught my dad how to bake bread. After he mastered that, he thought there was nothing he could not conquer in the kitchen. He decided to make a pie. Being a very frugal man, he didn't want to waste the last bit of shortening in the cup, so he melted it and added it to the flour. That was his first and last attempt at pie crust.

When my sister, Marian, was in the eighth grade, she took Home Economics. From that time on, she did all the cooking, and it was wonderful. She not only learned new recipes, but Home Economics in those days taught proper table setting and manners, which was a great help to my mom. In those days, no one left the table until they were dismissed, and that NEVER happened until my dad read a Bible story and we sang a hymn.

The history of developing civilizations show that family meals were an earmark of growth in a structured lifestyle. Respect for one another, exchanging ideas, sharing the events of the day, appreciating not only a good meal but the social skills needed in the ever-troubled world outside. After dinner, we worked together, clearing up the kitchen, singing with my sisters the songs we learned at school.

Snow on snow
with lovely whiteness everywhere
Moonlight is waking
to make the night more fair.
Life of mine

be peaceful like the winter's night
Sleeping or waking
as pure, as softly bright.

Good memories.

C.R. Baker

02-16-2007

Widowed

This Valentine's Day, I said, "Grow up. The past is the past," but I forgot to tell my friends. I received cards and calls from family, from Lynda, who was snowed-in, happy as a clam for the break. Rox had us "girls" over for a wonderful lunch to celebrate my anniversary, and I felt loved and contented in my "pleasant pastures".

03-23 ‹2007?›

What did I do this week that just made me laugh?

I read a really tempting recipe, so I assembled all the ingredients; easy recipe. I put it in the oven and then my neighbor came to critique this delicious dessert. Well, it fell 150 points below my expectations. What was there to do but nibble and squirt? We had fun, though; the storm sent her scurrying for home. The power cut off, so I thought, "Good, I'll just cuddle up and watch TV by candlelight." Right!

May 11, 2007

My mother was born on February 3, 1883 in Grand Haven, Michigan. Her parents were Jacob and Henrietta Dykstra. They named her Tetja (Tillie in English). She had one older sister, Ida. There were no middle names in those days. There were several other siblings to follow. Those who survived into adult years were three brothers and three sisters. When my mother was seven years old, her father died in a flu epidemic. Her mother eventually remarried, and the family moved to Holland, Michigan, where my mother met my Dad, Gerrit Dalman, at an April Fool's Day party. My dad was an amateur photographer, hired to take pictures at the party. They married on October 2. My mother's family migrated to California when I was three years old, leaving behind the two older sisters and their families.

I know nothing about the schools in that time. I do know that my mom was an avid reader and had picture-perfect Palmar-method penmanship.

My mother had black hair. It was common for a woman to go from birth to death without ever cutting their hair, which was true of my mother. I do remember watching her in the morning, brushing out the long hair, winding it "just so" into a rope that was twisted and secured in a bun at the back of her neck. My mother was the picture of health, slightly overweight, with a round, rosy face. She loved having babies, loved being pregnant, and, in that time of her life, was full of energy and happiness. The first of eleven babies was born at a hospital.

We were a healthy bunch. Mom's best friend was a Norwegian lady, the city health nurse. I couldn't possibly spell her name, but phonetically it sounded like "Miss Skirtchee". She was a frequent visitor at our home, and she and my mom shared a love for healthy living and a search for a Godly life. It was at that time that my mom started reading the Scofield Reference Bible, and her reading raised many questions about her heritage. Her hunger for perfection was insatiable, and she became alienated from the old Dutch church, which relied heavily on tradition and the wisdom of the Dominie, and she moved to a more Methodistic church with all of us in tow, including my reluctant father. This caused a big stir among all of our staunch Dutch relatives, and overnight, we moved from the norm in our community to a small minority, a radical social adjustment for us as children.

My mom loved the music in the Wesleyan Methodist church. Although, in moments of deep emotion, she would revert to the ponderous simplicity of the old Dutch psalms, which we didn't understand, but for her as with us, those old songs, which have seen us through many troubled times, became our "bulwark never failing". They were a gift of comfort straight from the throne of God. When I came home from school in the afternoon, I always knew where my mother was; I could hear her singing her favorite hymns.

It didn't help at all that my mother monitored everything that went on at school. She read every single book that we read, which is not such a great task when you consider that she only had to read the oldest child's book, which were recycled over and over again as younger children came up through the grades. I remember so well the day that I came home with my fourth-grade reading book. My mom said, "Oh! I like that book", and then proceeded to drop everything and read to us with great enjoyment, about the farmer who kept building farm buildings while the family was crammed into a little house. She read, laughing with delight, at the wife's revenge. My mother had no fear of the school board, and she jealously guarded what we were taught.

I have often wondered what caused my mom to have such a terrible fear of God. Her life was a constant flow of super highs followed by scary lows. She was quick-tempered but also had a great sense of humor. For example: She is the only person that I have ever known to be able to scold and laugh at the same time. One dark, windy night, when I was three or four years old, my two older brothers convinced their youngers sisters that newspapers blowing in the wind outside, were ghosts. We were terrified. Our screaming brought my mom flying up the stairs to the rescue. When she looked out the window and saw the papers looing and diving in the wind, she tried to scold my brothers, but she kept erupting in laughter. It was the laughter that convinced us that all was well.

There were a lot of rules in our home, and it seemed a desperate effort to measure up to an impossible standard. The house was never clean enough, and our behavior was often found wanting. My mother's volatile temper found me often hiding and frightened. The sunny times were beautiful but so temporary.

Table talk in our home was often about church politics or FDR, who was surely the Anti-Christ.

When I was a teenager, my cousin, who was a student at Hope College and prided himself on being agnostic, often came for Sunday evening supper. He loved to get my mom into arguments, and I listened to his point of view. It sounded so brilliant, so plausible, so sophisticated. My mom would get louder and louder as they argued, and I began to drift away from the absolutes of my mother's faith and look for something less scary.

April 16 *<2008?>*

Easter when I was a child was purely religious in our home. I remember the sunrise service and the feeling of joy in the air. Yes, there were bunnies and chocolate eggs, but not in our house. My father-in-law always gave my mother-in-law a large chocolate egg on Easter. I commented, often to my husband, how kind and thoughtful, but I never received a chocolate egg. My husband loved giving me just the right gift for other occasions. But to this day, I have yet to receive a chocolate egg.

04-17-2008

Dalman Thanksgiving

Holland, Michigan

When our children were small and we still lived in the area settled by our grandparents so many years ago, our clan always celebrated Thanksgiving together. We rented a gym so that the children had lots of room to play. We were a prolific bunch, and when we all got together in one place, it was quite a bash. My brother, from Kansas City and his crew of five, my sister, from Flint Michigan, another seven, a brother and wife from Texas, a brother from Denver, another five. Add to that all of us who still lived in the area. The roster read like the begats in the Old Testament.

Those who came from afar helped pay for the cost of the turkey and rental. We divided up the rest of the dinner between the households in the area. Nobody was terribly stressed out; we all had our favorite dishes. We all ate too much; we had a great time, happy to be together. But the dinner was just the beginning. After the feast was cleared away and the left-overs stashed into containers and the kitchen was as clean as when we arrived, we played Bingo. Everyone brought small gifts; it was an awesome mess. Windshield washer fluid, packs of cards, some used stuff, some white elephant gifts, some really nice things like candles or tapes of Christmas music, and just "stuff". And because the children played, too, there were lots of toys.

So, the games began. If you got a "bingo", you could pick anything you wanted. After a while, the gifts were gone, but we didn't stop there. If you won, you could go around and take whatever you wanted from someone who had already won it. You could win something and lose it several times before the game ended. It was fun because the children were as fiercely involved as their parents. You might try to hide something you would really like to keep, but the little kids had sharp eyes and loud voices about that. There was lots of laughter and kidding and groaning. It was such great fun.

All too soon, the night was passed, and it was time for "good-byes", hugs, and promises to write. Away went all the stuffed and tired parents and kids, their loot packed up to head for home or wherever they were staying. In later years, for us, it was a 125-mile ride back to Indiana. It was worth every mile, and as we drove through the night, we were already looking forward to next year.

Carolyn Baker

June 2008

In Michigan

Every spring, as a child, I remember the return of the birds, the competition to see the first robin, the first blue bird, the first red-winged black bird. All winter long, we had faithfully fed the sparrows, and the return of the colors of the summer population always meant the cold, sluggish winter was over, and the bright colors of the birds soon would be duplicated in the arrival of flowers deep in the woods, waiting for our hike to gather.

June 2008

THE WORM AND I

"Summertime when the living is easy" …well not really. All summer long, our family worked hard at preserving food for the winter months ahead. No freezers in those days. The produce from my dad's garden and the fruits purchased from numerous peddlers eventually found its way into the storage room in our basement.

I can still picture my mother standing in that room in late October, surveying with a look of serene satisfaction, the fruit of her labor. The jam cupboard was crammed full, shelves and miscellaneous tables loaded with jars of stewed tomatoes, pickles, relishes, apple sauce, pears, and cherries for pie. It was a beautiful sight.

One particular day in mid-August stands out in my memory. One of my mom's favorite peddlers had come that day with his flatbed truck, loaded with the first picking of Red Haven peaches. We bought three bushels, and their delicate aroma graced the whole house. The next day, we would have a festive canning bee in our kitchen; but that night, for dessert, we were to have a sampling of the best peaches ever grown.

In our good Dutch home, we always had prayer before a meal. All eyes closed, no peeking. The penalty for peeking was no dessert. But I was just a kid, six or seven years old, and I peeked. To my horror, I saw a small white worm with a black nose, leisurely inching its way up the side of a peach and disappearing down the other side. I panicked. What should I do?

Those were the days before sprays controlled pesky worms. Luscious, wholesome fruits and vegetables proliferated side by side with wiggly worms. That was the way it was, but worms made me feel squeamish, especially in food. UGH! What a disgusting dilemma!

I had to do something.

If I told them, they would know I had peeked. If I didn't tell them, someone might eat that worm. It might even be in my serving. My stomach rebelled at the thought. I had to tell them. My taste buds clamored, "Don't tell"; my conscience whispered, "Tell."

Because the memory of that day in August comes back to me so warm and sweet, with no lurking shadows of regret, I think I warned them. I think the heavy scepter of justice was waived; mercy was granted, and I had dessert.

Carolyn Baker

May 02, 2009

Camping at Ottawa Beach

One June day, I remembered my high school days when my school friends took the first week of vacation camping at Ottawa Beach, but my mother wouldn't let me do that…too much hanky-panky, etc.

I mentioned it to Gordon, and he said, "let's go." In one hour, we were on our way. A two-hour drive and we were setting up a borrowed tent, and we just inhaled deeply the Lake Michigan air. The bliss of being again at the playground of our dating days was wonderful, and then we realized that we were two retired people, dead center in a mob of teenagers. We wondered if we would get any sleep, but we did. The rules were strictly enforced, and we felt like we were young again. The next day, we tidied up our camp and left to see friends and family.

While we were gone, a storm came up, which blew down our tent and soaked all our belongings. We spent two hours cleaning up. We packed the car and headed for Russ's and checked into a motel.

December 2, 2009

I have kept cherished memories for all these years because they bring to mind the good things that happened during a round and difficult time in my life.

I was the sixth child (fourth daughter) in a large family, but an older sister became our church leader, bringing happy times almost out of nothing.

Christmas 1932: No tree. Marian arranged boxes to form a fake fireplace and covered it with paper with a red brick pattern – went out to the woods for pieces of wood – using red paper to imitate a fire. When viewed through half-closed eyes, we could almost believe that it was real.

1932: No money. Not to fear, Marian helped us make gifts: Pin cushions from scraps of cloth, vases from discarded jars covered with envelope liners from last year's cards. We had piles of small gifts, some of them our own precious toys. I can still see my mother laughing over still another potholder.

CHAPTER THREE:

Family Fun — Originally Compiled by Carolyn in 2006 as a Christmas Gift to Her Children

Family Fun

Carolyn Bouman Baker

MOM'S COLLECTION OF FUNNY MEMORIES

To All My Children,

It has been so much fun to recall all the good times we have shared over the years. The other day, in writing class, we were asked to finish the sentence, "My happiest moment this week was...." I thought of my call to Lynda to ask her what she remembered about our family jokes. She reminded me of things I had forgotten, and I sat there rocking with laughter as we talked about the fun times. She mentioned the small, red balloons she and Dan tied on Dan and Jerry Shepherd's half-grown tomato plants. When I said I had forgotten that, Lynda asked how that could be since I was the one who helped blow up the balloons. We laughed about my sure-fire way to get Dan up in the morning: just plant one stress-loaded thought in his mind. For example, I would say, "They are waiting." And he would come stumbling down the stairs, "Who? What? Where?"

How could we forget Dan's eighteenth birthday party?! Lynda had tipped over a dining room chair and covered it with a blanket to make a bench and motioned for Dan to sit next to her on the chair back. She did a spoof of an interview, congratulating him on Boy Scout activities and his trophy for the Junior High Ping Pong Tournament. Then, she asked him what he wanted to be when he grew up. He thought anything out of doors would be fine. At that moment, she jumped up with a hurried "Just a second, I forgot something", and sent all six feet of Dan's spruced-up, dignified self, sprawling to the floor.

Lynda was the pro in orchestrating a prank. When she and Bill lived in Iceland, she had a very proper friend who bragged about never being caught in a practical joke. Lynda and a girlfriend had great fun arranging for this guy to pick up a cake from the girlfriend's house and deliver it to Lynda's house for a party. Of course, there was no cake in that pan, just a couple of books securely wrapped and taped. When the doorbell rang and the guy handed the cake to Lynda, she dramatically dropped it. He was mortified. Lynda's accomplice, waiting on the phone, joined in the raucous laughter; and he suddenly realized his bragging days were over.

Funny things happen around us all the time. They aren't planned, but in a flash there they are. Some people are gifted in recognizing humor, and in a moment, a dull day is brightened with laughter. There is something so refreshing in a humorous retort; like a flash of sunshine, it eases the daily grind.

I am thinking of that late afternoon in Zeeland. I had been hard at work all day and was cleaning in the far bedroom when I heard Dad coming up the stairs into the dark hallway where I had left a pail of water. I called a warning out to him, "Don't kick the bucket!" He shot back, "Perish the thought."

I remember the day in Zeeland when Dad and Dan had inadvertently purchased the same pair of shoes at the local shoe store. I looked over at Dad putting his size eight and a half foot into Dan's size ten shoe. The look on his face was priceless. I started to laugh, and then everybody came to see what was so funny. Dan didn't plan that scene, but as we all stood there laughing, I was filled with the warm knowledge that we had fostered a family capable of laughing at ourselves. Priceless.

One day, when we lived in Creston, Illinois, Jack came home with an assignment to present a new word to his eighth-grade class. He asked for help. I thought the word "horrendous" would be appropriate. He looked the word up, and we talked about it until I felt certain he understood. The next morning, as the yellow bus was coming down the road and Jack was flying out the door, I called after him, "What's the word?" He looked back at me with a blank stare, and then started hitting the side of his head, saying, "hor... hor... hor." I waited all day for that dreaded phone call. When he came home, I asked him if his teacher liked his new word. He grumbled, "My teacher never heard of the word "hor".

Jack, of course, takes the prize for impromptu humor. His mutterings from the back seat of the car often turned tension into wild laughter. For a short time, the five of us sang together for special music renditions. Jack's quick wit and Sam's infectious laughter brought an end to that. I think the song that ended it was the one with the excuse I s for not coming to the banquet. Instead of singing, "I have married a wife, I have bought me a cow...", Jack sang, "I have married a cow, I have bought me a wife", and sent Sam into uncontrolled giggles and peals of laughter. Exit stage left the Von Bouman Family Singers.

Then there was the day in Tucson when Dad and I were stopped at a red light on Broadway. A couple in the car ahead of us was chatting away when the light changed. They didn't move. Dad hit the horn and then with the instincts of a professional driver, Dad made sure he passed that car before the next light. We were first in line, but it was a long light and we were talking when we heard a horn blast behind us. It was the same couple, laughing and waving at us. We laughed with them. They had turned irritation into fun. What a gift.

Now, the next generation is into the game, and it is so much fun to watch them. Susie shared with me Allyson's peace offering to her future Father-in-law, Mark, after he reprimanded the viola section for "cutting up" during rehearsal. She gave him a package of Oreo cookies, in which all the frosting had been replaced with good stuff like horseradish, mayonnaise, mustard, butter, jalapeños, and tartar sauce.

Center stage last Christmas was my great grandson, Tennyson, crawling around under the table as we played cards. He eyed some bare toes and thought to tickle them, but giggled so hard in anticipation that he couldn't do it. I do not need to be a prophet to read his future.

In this little booklet, I have shared some of my favorite memories with you. I know there are many stories left for you to tell, and I hope you will do just that. Humor is such a good medicine, and I hope you will cultivate it all the days of your life. I believe humor falls under the heading of "Whatsoever things are lovely, whatsoever things are true, whatsoever things are just, think on those things."

I am so thankful that God purposely gave each of you to Dad and me. I am wealthy with good memories of the past and so blessed with your love for me right now. I thank each of you for the way you have delighted, and sometimes cared for me, and often made me howl with glee. I would like to close with the last lines of a favorite poem. I don't recall the title or the author, but it ends like this:

Give me a sense of humor, Lord
Give me the grace to see a joke
To get happiness out of life
And pass it on to other folk.

Love to all,

And a Merry Christmas

Mom (2006)

Faulty Plumbing on Center Street

I loved that old house, but being an old house, it had some quirks. Namely, if you took a shower, and someone in the kitchen turned on the hot water, the shower ran COLD.

Being civilized people, when we took a shower, we asked everyone to please not turn on the hot water in the kitchen. I guess, one time, I forgot and gave Sam a bit of a shock.

One particular Saturday morning, Sam warned me that he was about to take a shower. I said, "Ok." Then he fooled around for a while, warned me again, but still didn't get to it. When, for the third time, he said, "Please do **not** turn on the hot water", it ticked me off. So, when I heard the shower running, I turned on the hot water. What a shock!! Sam had aimed the spray right at my middle and taped it open. I yelped and jumped back in a hurry, right into Sam, who stood there laughing. He had just been waiting to rush out and watch the fun. He knew if he begged me enough, I would retaliate. He got me!

C.R.B.

Baltimore/Washington Airport, June 2005

I had a wonderful visit with Jack and his family, but now it was time to get back to the reality of summer in Tucson.

Jack secured a pass so he could be with me until I boarded my plane. He wheeled me down the concourse like he owned the place as we enjoyed our last bit of time together. We approached a man on a bench parallel to the walkway. He was sitting with his newspaper opened up in front of his face. Jack said, "Just wait a minute", pulled up to within a few feet of the man, and started reading the backside of the man's paper. I didn't dare breathe or move a muscle. If the man had dropped the paper, we would have been eye to eye. Jack just stood behind me, calmly reading the headlines, then casually moved away.

"Jack!" I said. "Don't ever do that again!" He said, "Do what?" grinning at me with his look of angelic innocence. I said…well, never mind what I said.

When we got to the boarding area, Jack asked the attendant if he could wheel me down the ramp. The attendant refused but informed us it would be 20 or 30 minutes before boarding and Jack could stay until it was time for me to go. What a wonderful time we had as we talked about our family, the grandchildren, and our hopes for them. Then we prayed together, just like Jack was maybe, possibly, a normal, grown up, serious person. But no!! The attendant came, we said our "goodbyes", and then as we started down the ramp, Jack called after me, "Mom, do you have enough Kleenex?" A few seconds later, his voice reverberated down the runway again, "Mom, don't talk to any strangers." …" Mom, go right home." …" Mom, don't forget to call me." All these reminders, such an integral part of our farewells when he was younger, were called back to me as I tried to shrink into the seat of the wheelchair, and the spectators laughed harder and harder at every sally. Just as I rounded the corner, I heard one last call with a different tone in his voice, "MOM, I LOVE YOU!"

The helpers at the bottom of the ramp cheered and yelled back at Jack, "We love you, too."

How could they help it?

C.R.B.

The "Don't Touch" Box of Chocolates

Christmas 2004 at Lynda's home in Anderson, Indiana

All the ingredients for a perfect Christmas were in place: the snow, the beautiful decorations, the gifts piled high, the traditional food, and best of all, the children (two toddlers and a four-month old charmer, who thought we were all ridiculously funny).

Lynda had finally sent all 23 of her 4th graders off for the holidays and she was home at last, loaded with gifts from their parents. Most of the loot was snacks, cookies, jars of various mixes, candies, you name it…it was there. The snack bar in her kitchen was resplendent.

But there was one box that was not to be opened. Lynda knew there were chocolates in the box because another teacher had received the same gift. It was so beautifully wrapped that Lynda placed it on the coffee table as part of the Christmas décor.

After a few days, Jim and Nina started hinting that we should sample the chocolates; but Lynda, with children in the house, was in teacher mode. Using her LAW CAST IN CONCRETE voice, she mandated that the box was **not** to be opened. We were down to about the last two days of Jim and Nina's visit, and there was a lot of kidding about the box, but Lynda was adamant.

One night, I secretly mentioned to Nina that we should open the box and fill it with stones. Her mouth dropped, and she laughingly confessed that it had been done. Jim had taken the box into their bathroom, and with the door locked, had carefully unwrapped it, taken out the trays of chocolates, substituted them with carefully weighed books and socks, then meticulously rewrapped it, good as new.

Our last evening there, as we settled down to our umpteenth game of Hand and Foot, I declared I was not leaving until we opened the box. That did it. There had been three extra adults and three extra little ones in the house for a week, and the threat of a sit-down strike broke our Mrs. Bergin's back! Lynda carefully undid the lovely wrappings, lifted the lid, and let out a shriek. "You ate the chocolates!" she wailed. Nina quickly grabbed her, assured her that all was safe, and rushed the trays of candy out of the bedroom. And Lynda, she who has pulled her full share of pranks over the years, got some of her own medicine, while Nina, Jim, and I had a delicious time savoring the moment… and some of the best chocolates ever.

C.R.B.

Fourth of July

July was the time of year for catching perch in Lake Michigan. If the perch were running, a person could get his limit of 50 before 10 am, but this was not the day. Dad was out on the lake with all his gear at the crack of dawn. He knew all the tricks but got nary a nibble. So, he headed for home, ready for a nap.

The family was still sleeping upstairs when he got home, so he crashed on the sofa, which was directly across from the front door. He left the door open to catch any possible breeze on a very hot, muggy morning. We got up. He didn't stir. The kids went out to play. They ran in and out several times while he snoozed in just his briefs. I threw a sheet over him, but he threw it off. It was getting late and my fold often dropped in on holidays. He just mumbled when I tried to wake him, so what was I to do?

I did it.

I picked the sheet up off the floor. Then, I went to Jack and Mary's next door. I asked them to come to our front door, wait for the phone to ring, and then knock as loudly as they could. He would not answer the door in his briefs, and he could not get to the phone without being seen.

Oh my! You could have heard him holler, "CAROL…CAROL…CAROL" from a block away.

He forgave me…but not right away.

C.R.B.

Lil's Barbecue's One Pinochle Night

Playing Pinochle at the Shepards' one evening, the guys decided they wanted barbecue sandwiches from Lil's Drive-In down at the "Y". It was 9:45 and Lil's closed at 10:00, so they ran for the car, telling us to call and place an order.

Mary dialed the number – busy. She dialed again – busy (old rotary phone, no automatic redial). She kept dialing. Busy, busy, busy! It was 9:50, still "busy". It was 9:54, still "busy". I offered to dial while she held the receiver. After a couple of tries, I saw the emergency numbers posted on the wall. So, just to break the monotony, I dialed the police department.

"Oh good", Mary said, "it's ringing!" With her face registering shock, she banged the receiver down with her usual three explosive words for me when she got caught, "YOU D__ F___!!!"

C.R.B.

Pelicans

It was August of 1990, and Dad and I were headed home to Tucson after a two-month stay with Dan in British Columbia. Our first night out, we stayed in Eugene, Oregon, and then from there we turned west over the Coastal Range and south down the Pacific Coast Highway. It was a truly beautiful drive, and we never tired of looking at the ocean. We camped on the beach one night in Northern California. What a treat!

As we approached San Diego, we began seeing this strange bird; it had a long, pointed beak protruding like a sword out in front of it with a goiter-like appendage flapping below the beak. It was as large as a turkey and had a wing-span of 50 or 60 inches. To the eyes of someone from the upper mid-west, they were a wonderment. I pointed it out to Dad, but I guess he was too busy driving to be impressed.

Soon, I saw the birds flying in formation, three of them flying like dive-bombers peeling off one after the other, headfirst into the crashing surf. They were catching fish! I gasped at their precision and skill. What a sight! I exclaimed, "Did you see that?" Dad enthusiastically replied, "Guy Yah! She hardly had anything on at all!"

C.R.B.

The Hardware Store Caper

Creston, Illinois 1968

It was early evening, and I need to make a trip to a hardware store on the outskirts of DeKalb, Illinois. Jack asked if he could ride along. I said, "Sure." Jack was always good company. It had been raining, so I grabbed a raincoat, one of those olive-green things purchased from the Army Surplus store.

The store was busy, and I needed to find several things, so Jack wandered off, hunting me up every now and then to see how I was doing. Whenever he found me, he would poke me, point out things, pat me, thank me for taking him along, take my arm, or straighten out my collar. I couldn't figure out what had gotten into the kid.

People seemed to be very friendly that night, smiling broadly at us. Jack would smile back; in fact, he never stopped smiling.

At last, I finished, and Jack helped me push the cart to the front of the store. As we stood in line, the people behind us were chuckling and talking about something funny. But it wasn't until the girl at the checkout looked at me and started to laugh, that I realized Jack had plastered me with price stickers. They were all up and down my back and down my sleeves, because every time he touched me, I got another one.

That prank could not be duplicated in this day and age. Our sophisticated bar code and scanner system takes care of that. But I can assure you that if I were to go to the store with Jack today, he would find some way to make people laugh, and probably at my expense.

C.R.B.

Practical Jokes, Quips, and Pranks

April Fool's Day is usually the time for elaborate hoaxes and tricks, but in our family, hoaxes and tricks seemed to be an impromptu thing and would erupt all year long. It was a fun way of probing the foibles of family and friends. Usually, the victim would set the stage.

My dad's sisters were so very, very proper (their foible). Once, when my folks were getting ready to spend an evening with his family, Dad laid the end of a thread loosely on his sleeve, connected of course to a spool in his pocket. How he laughed when one of his very proper sisters came to helpfully pull it off. Dad's practical jokes were never mean, just gentle fun. And so, he laid the groundwork for generations of pranks to follow.

After I married, we lived next door to our best friends, Jack and Mary Shepard. They had moved to our little Dutch town to start a business and, eager to blend in with the community, were very conscious of appearances. Our two families lived on one end of a short street with six or seven houses to the north. Jack was the last in the neighborhood to leave for work in the morning. It was almost too easy to take their Christmas tree, which had been sitting next to the

79

dumpster in the backyard for almost four months, and bring it up to the front of the house. We propped a large sign against it: FOR SALE CHEAP! All the neighbors saw it before Jack left for work in the morning. Gotcha!

Backlash. When our mail was delivered in the early afternoon, we received a box labeled, "Chicken Dinner." It contained some chicken feed and a lot of chicken dirt.

That was the beginning of several fun-filled years, bantering back and forth. Our children were the same age, and we spent many long evenings playing Pinochle while our kids camped out on each other's sofas. Not much money for sitters in those days.

There was a hatchery down the street, which supplied baby chicks to the farmers in the area. The hatchery would sort out sub-standard chicks to be disposed of. The children in the neighborhood loved to pick up these cast-off chicks and raise them. Many a city girl was excited about the prospect of raising the chicks her children brought home. She bought some of the best chicken feed, fixed a good shelter, watered them, and couldn't wait for them to start laying eggs. At six weeks, she was getting very impatient, so just for the fun of it, I put an egg into the prepared straw nest. She was so happy. She called the hatchery, she called neighbors; she was overjoyed. Of course, she now expected to gather an egg or two every day. I put another egg in the nest. One day, Mary asked what she could feed her chicks to get brown eggs, as she really preferred brown eggs. I went to Ten Harmsel's Market and bought one brown egg, thinking, "Enough already." I hard-boiled it, chuckling to myself as I pictured her face when she tried to crack it open.

Backlash. The joke was on me. Mary knew it was a prank after the second egg and had just been egging me on.

C.R.B.

Summer Nights

Those low ceilings of our upstairs bedrooms in Holland, Michigan were so oppressive, especially when there was absolutely no air moving. If it got really, really hot, my mom would let us girls throw our mattresses down over the railing from upstairs and set up camp on the screened-in front porch.

This all had to be done without waking the younger ones. We were strictly forbidden to make any noise out there. Not a peep! After my oldest sister (who was supposed to keep us in line) went to sleep, we younger girls would play tag on the ceiling using pieces of mirror reflecting off the streetlight. It was crazy, wild fun. We smothered our laughter in the pillows and got hotter than ever, but we were never caught.

One night, we decided to sleep on the upstairs deck out back with no screening and no streetlights. We had just gotten nicely settled when we realized that the neighborhood bully was up in the tree about 15 feet from the deck, watching us. Marian slipped downstairs and told my folks. My dad went out the front door, hooked up the hose, and before the kid knew what was happening, began watering the tree. My dad sprayed that tree with nice, cold water for a good 15 minutes. The bully never made a peep and stayed right up in that tree until my dad went in. I wonder how the boy (maybe 15 years old) explained his drenching to his folks.

C.R.B.

Sunday Evening Service in our Humble Little Zeeland, Michigan Church

Our little Zeeland church was humble. The seats, purchased from an old theater, were fold-down seats with wrought iron armrest supports. Jack was old enough that year to attend the evening service with us. He was being very good that night, not his usual fidgety six-year old self.

As the pastor finished his sermon and was about to announce the closing hymn, I glanced down to find that Jack had knotted the ribbon belt of the dress

I was wearing to the armrest supports. I had about ten seconds to get it loose before the "Rise, please" would find me still seated and tied down to the seat.

The people around us were aware and stifled their laughter while I struggled with the knots. Fortunately, six-year olds aren't good at tight knots.

You almost got me that time, Jack.

C.R.B.

The Kellner's Christmas Tree Trick

The ancient artificial Christmas tree was up. It dated back to the early years of Susie and Mark's marriage; and the accumulation of precious ornaments, rich in memories, were hung carefully to hide the bone, skinny branches. The children loaded the lower branches with their favorites; many of the ornaments were of their own making and treasured by all. The higher branches were filled in with enough glitter and Christmas glamour to fool even the most critical eye. The Kellner tradition of videotaping was in process to mark the year of growth in the children, when someone started singing the family version of "Tannenbaum".

Oh Christmas tree, oh Christmas tree

How shiny is thy vinyl

All red and green with twinkly lights

As Christmas-y as flying kites

Oh Christmas tree, oh Christmas tree

All is forgiven; you're fireproof.

Every year, Mark and Susie vowed that next year, they would get a new tree; but once again, Christmas was upon them and there stood old faithful… one more time.

A few days before Christmas, Mark happened upon a big, beautiful, full-branched, artificial tree in one of the stores. The price had been cut drastically for a quick, late sale. He bought the tree, hiding it in the back of the station wagon.

That night, after they were sure all the children were sound asleep, they took down the old tree. Using the video, Mark and Susie assembled the new tree, replacing each ornament and all trimmings exactly where the children had put them. After hours of labor, they finally finished. They could hardly wait for the reaction of the children. What would they think? Zachary was ten, Natalie, eight, and Abi, five. How would they explain the height and width of the new tree? Mark and Susie didn't get much sleep that night, anticipating the fun they would have listening to the children's surprise about the tree that "grew" overnight.

Early the next morning, Zachary and Natalie looked at the tree with dumbfounded wonder. Then, the speculating began. Zachary thought his parents had put higher boxes under the tree. Natalie said no, they must have watered it to make it grow. How could everything look just as it had the night before but be so much bigger? They couldn't agree. Soon, the commotion woke Abi and baby Gillian. Mark and Susie jumped out of the shadows and laughingly explained the mystery.

This was not only a practical joke; it was also an extravagant labor of love, just to give their children a happy surprise.

C.R.B.

Volkswagen Years 1961-1970

Three little kids in the back seat of a faded orange 1957 Volkswagen waiting for the light to change. Three teenagers having fun in a big, souped-up car, waiting for the light to change. The stage was set, and the kids started urging, "Do it, Dad! Do it!" Dad revved the motor a couple of times. Dad looked at the other car with a raised eyebrow. They looked down on us with scorn. Of course, they could beat us across that intersection. The light changed. The souped-up car streaked across the intersection while Dad lazily shifted into second gear and chugged, chugged to the other side, while the kids howled with glee, "You got 'em, Dad, you got 'em."

Three little kids in the back seat of an **anthracite grey Volkswagen**, traveling across country to see their big sister, Lynda, in college. We sang songs, rounds, hymns, choruses, and silly songs. WE made up new words to old tunes and never tired of the fun. One of the kids' favorites was singing "Leaning on Jesus", as they swayed to the music.

We decided to stop for something to drink, so we told them to put on their shoes. Sam couldn't find one of his shoes and Susie said in her sweet, mothering voice, "Well, now, let's see; where were you last?"

Three growing children packed into the back seat of a **jet-black Volkswagen** late in the afternoon, heading out to Hubble's Cottage for the evening. It was hot, no air conditioning, and the children were tired. The traffic was heavy as we worked our way through the southern edge of Grand Haven. Finally, we cleared out of the traffic, up that last little incline, and there it was, the beautiful expanse of Lake Michigan. Out of the back seat, Jack's voice exploded, "Good for you, Dad. I knew you could do it!"

Leaning on the fender of our tan 1967 square-back Volkswagen, Sam was sobbing uncontrollably. We had just returned from the vet, where his problem cat was to be put to sleep for biting a neighbor girl. Sam's friends gathered around and tried to console him, but nothing helped.

Fifteen minutes later, I saw Sam playing with his friends, happy and laughing. I asked him what had happened. He said, "I know I'm not supposed to play with that kid Rob. I know he uses bad words, but he is my friend and now I own half of his cat."

C.R.B.

The Hamburger Thief

Shortly after our family moved from Michigan to Northern Illinois, big brother Dan came home on Spring Break. His siblings, five, eight, and eleven years old adored him, as they should; he was a wonderful big brother. One Saturday afternoon, we all piled into the car to drive around and show Dan the new places we had discovered. Our last stop was The Little Red School House, our favorite hamburger place.

As we sat down to eat, Dan said, "Oops, forgot the catsup." As Dad quickly jumped up to get it, Dan took Dad's sandwich, took a huge bite out of it, and then wrapped it up again, getting it back in place with not a second to spare. The kids looked at Dan with awe. How dare he do that and…oh boy this was going to be fun.

Dad asked the blessing while Dan tried not to choke on all that food in his mouth, and we desperately tried to suppress the giggles. When Dad opened his hamburger, he roared, "WHAT IN THE WORLD?!" He jumped up and charged to the counter. We couldn't hear what he said, but his body language was explicit.

At first, the man at the counter looked perplexed, but then, looking over Dad's shoulder, he pointed at us all doubled over with laughter. Dad, who was fond of pulling jokes himself, knew that *he* had been caught for a change. He had about 20 steps back to our table to figure out how he was going to handle this. With a grin, Dan handed him his own untouched burger saying, Gotcha, Dad." Dad couldn't resist the infectious laughter of his family. By this time, all the guys behind the counter were laughing as well; so being a good sport, he joined in the fun.

Sycamore, Illinois, 1967

C.R.B.

MY NOSE

I have an incontinent nose
Like a faucet it drips and it flows
I've petitioned Depends
For a product that ends
The drip from my lip to my toes

A COLD GONE BAD

Oh the struggle
Of a cold gone bad
Resident in bronchi
And phlegm filled head
Together we sail
This hacking sea
Till I get rid of it
Or it gets rid of me

MISS ME

You say you will miss me
I'm sure you will
But not for love engendered
You say you will miss me
You can bet on that
For loss of services rendered

DUST DEVIL

Hey! You dizzy dust devil
Twirling in the sun
Do you think
You are the only one
Having any fun?
Well! I'll dance to my music
And you can dance to yours
Just stay away from my house
When I am out of doors.

C.R.B.

CHAPTER FOUR:

A Day of Infamy, A Day of Victory: Recollections of World War II

December 7, 1941: A Day of Infamy
August 15, 1945: A Day of Victory

When Japan bombed Pearl Harbor, the repercussions rattled every window in every home, every school, every church, and every business in America. Nothing was the same after that "Day of Infamy". I was 19 years old that year, a young bride full of dreams and now full of uncertainty.

The economy, in a slow recovery from the Great Depression, went into a frantic rush to tool up for the needs of a nation at war. All the cars, refrigerators, stoves, toasters, alarm clocks, washing machines, and all the civilized necessities we are now accustomed to were no longer available. Those factories now produced guns, ammo, jeeps, tanks, housing, schools, hospitals, clothing, and healthcare for the military. The labor force for all of this was depleted, as men were pulled into the service. The women hung up their dishtowels, and with the help of neighbors and grandparents to care for their children, joined the war effort by working in the factories. And the song "Rosie the Riveter" was born.

Early in the war, I worked for Fafner, a company that had once made floor registers but was then retooled to produce ball bearings for the government. I worked at a bench using a gauge to insure proper ratios in the finished product.

Later, I worked for Lear Avia, the company that developed the first "Bombsight". I, along with several others, worked in Material Control, keeping track of everything that entered the plant and exactly where it could be found at any given time. This was done with a simple double entry method but in an office without a single adding machine.

Toward the end of the war, I worked for a short while in the General Motors standing plant, that had in peacetime produced auto bodies but then made shell casings. That was a fun job. I drove a three-wheeled tow motor with a half inch steel plate body. We pulled racks of shells from one place to another, we pulled bins of scrap to the trash area, and then the war was almost over, all the tow motor drivers and presses by pushing or pulling them an inch at a time. And that is what I did in the great war.

During those long war years, this country was no longer a happy-go-lucky place to live. There were constant reminders that we were at war from numerous gold stars hanging in the front windows of families that had lost a son or daughter in the war to the black-out drills, to skimpy gas rationing and the 35 mile per hour speed limit everywhere. Hitchhiking became a way of life for many. We felt perfectly safe stopping to give a lift.

Many necessities were rationed: sugar, shortening, butter, and oleo, which was white with a small blister pack of yellow food coloring to mix it ourselves. We saved grease, straining it into cans for recycling, we grew victory gardens, canning what we could and sharing with others the overflow. There were no home freezers available.

And then there were shortages; they could happen out of the blue. One year, there was not a potato to be found from spring to the fall harvest. Meat was iffy; you were fortunate if you had a butcher for a friend. But we coped. We wore rayon hose that wrinkled no matter what you did. Nylons were nonexistent. There were no rubber pants for babies, but we knit woolen yarn into soakers and it worked fine.

There were no weather reports from the day war was declared until the peace treaty was signed. We watched barometers and learned to read the sky.

The government advertised broadly the sale of war bonds to raise money for the war. Their signs and slogans were everywhere. I also remember vividly one sign that warned "Loose Lips Sink Ships."

But there was also a vitality in the land, a feeling of unity and courage. Patriotism was in full bloom and our world was worth whatever it took to preserve it. A whole generation of young people was decimated to stop the power struggle in Europe and the ruthless advances of Japan on our holdings in the South Pacific. Even though my mother was sure that Roosevelt was the Anti-Christ, she knew that the evil had to be stopped and there was a prayer in our home and in the churches and in the schools, that God would help us to bring an end to the horribleness of war. Every day, every week, every year the losses in human life and property mounted, and it began to feel like it would NEVER end.

When Germany surrendered, we thought that now it would be over, but the war in the Pacific carried on with brutal force. Don Bouman was aboard the destroyer, The Collett, in the final days of the war. He reported, "Our ship intercepted a message that was going from Tokyo to Washington, asking to end the war. But they were not ready for a complete surrender. The United States and our allies told them there would be nothing accepted except a full surrender. It was another month or so before that happened.

I remember hearing a newscast about a bomb so huge that if dropped onto the New York Harbor, it would empty it out of water. I heard it but didn't grasp the magnitude of this bomb. We did know that the Allies had assembled the largest armada in history in the South Pacific, but the Japanese were ready to fight to the last man. Their culture demanded it.

When the first Atom Bomb was dropped, we cringed at the devastation and prayed that the slaughter of our men and their men would stop, but days passed, and the killing went on. The second Atom Bomb finally convinced them to surrender.

When at last the war ended, the Battleship Missouri sailed into Tokyo Harbor and anchored not far from Don's ship. The final signing of the papers, the declaration ending the war, and the Japanese's full surrender was made on the bow of the Missouri. Don said that through binoculars, he was able to watch the whole thing. He could see the expressions on their faces and the kind of clothes they wore. A real thrill for a man who had not set foot on land for three and a half years. He was ready to come home.

We lived in Grand Rapids, Michigan at that time. Our Lynda was two years old. We heard on the radio that there was to be a big celebration in Campau Square that evening, and we decided to go. We knew better than to drive, so we took the bus as close as we could get. With Lynda on her dad's shoulders, we joined the mob in downtown Grand Rapids. It was shoulder-to-shoulder rejoicing, hugging, crying, laughing, and sharing with strangers about those we knew and their part in the terrible struggle. There were no political differences or color lines in that crowd; we were just one happy mob overflowing with thanksgiving and joy that it was finally over, and we had persevered to the end. Our Day of Victory. August 15, 1945.

CHAPTER FIVE:

Personal Letters

2010

Sam's 49th Birthday

Dear Sam,

HAPPY 49th BIRTHDAY.

I remember well the day you were born. It was a typical March day in late winter with lots of snow still on the ground. Nature was reluctant to give way to spring and you, three weeks overdue, were reluctant to make your appearance. Dr. Vander Wal assured me that all was well and said that he would induce labor if necessary, on the 18th of March. He also talked to me about having a natural birth without drugs. He said that every birth is such a wonderful experience but that most mothers preferred to avoid the pain and were unaware of the wonder of it all. I gulped and said that I would try. He promised that I could have help at any time.

I was told to check in at the Zeeland Hospital on Saturday the 18th at 8:30 pm. I was not to eat anything after lunch.

When the big day finally arrived, Dad and I decided to spend some time alone, just the two of us. Our first stop would be in Grand Haven. The pizza craze had just started in our area. Where we lived, there were no places serving pizza during the day, but we knew that Fabiano's in Grand Haven was open, so away we went.

Returning home, we took Lake Shore Drive to the Oval at Ottawa Beach. Over the winter, the waves, splashing and spraying, built up huge icebergs. The accumulation of ice, sometimes as big as small houses, was awesome to see. We parked and talked about the days ahead. At that time, they could not predict the sex of an unborn baby, but I was sure this baby was a girl. We decided that your name would be Rebecca. We wondered what it would be like to watch you graduate from high school when we were 57. We supposed that we might be using canes by then.

That was the way we spent your last day in hiding.

The nurse who checked me in that night was humming "Thank you Lord for saving my soul." Wow! That was *MY* special song!

You were born just before midnight, and I was wide awake. Dr. Vander Wal was very pleased with me, and he was right. It was a real thrill to have a clear mind, to hear your first cry, and to finally see your face. You weighed in at eight pounds and one ounce. You resembled Dan when he was born, and my heart was flooded with joy.

[Stage left Rebecca!]

We scrambled for just the right name for you, vacillating between Andrew or Samuel. We chose Samuel because there was an older man in our church who was such a dear man; we named you after him. Years later, we named a collie puppy, Becky, and then six or seven years later, you puzzled over what we would have named the dog if you had been a girl.

Sam, your birth was different than the others because in 1958, Dad and I became Christians; before that, we had two good friends, our neighbors Jack and Mary Shepard. They were the only people who visited me when Susie was born. When we started going to the Baptist church, they were disgusted with us and our friendship was over. When you were born, the whole Baptist church (small church) rejoiced with us and my room overflowed with visitors. When we came home, they brought in meals and showered us with cards. You certainly got a royal welcome.

In 1962, the *PILL* was born; no surprise babies. Good for you Sam; you made it "just under the wire."

You were our bonus gift from God, and I will be forever grateful. I pray that this new year in your life will be awesome, blessed by God in every way.

With all my love, Mom.

10-09

Dear Lynda,

I am so glad that you reminded me of those days long ago when you were praying for your wayward parents and you thought God wasn't listening. I thank you from the bottom of my heart for your faithful prayers, and I want to share with you what God was up to while you were praying, and He appeared to be deaf.

First off, I remember when you were almost four, we prayed with you when we tucked you in for the night. One night, you prayed earnestly that we would go to visit Grandma the next day, and then your eyes popped open and you said, "May we?" You knew God was up there somewhere, but permission came from your parents.

We moved to Zeeland, Michigan when you were six and Dan was two. We didn't attend church in those days. We slept in on Sunday mornings, and when you were a little older, you were allowed to get up to fix your own breakfast… and to listen to the radio. How well I remember Aunt Bertha's voice, from Radio Bible Class in Grand Rapids, splitting the early morning air. I pulled the covers over my ears, knowing that you were listening to a nice program.

Sundays for us were pleasant; Dad puttered around the house, doing little chores, or he would wander next door to the Shepards to visit with Jack and Mary. I usually spent a leisurely morning fixing a traditional Sunday Dinner with all the fixings. I enjoyed setting a festive table and making Sunday special.

I don't remember how old you were when you started writing and receiving mail from some of your radio programs. I thought it was a little precocious but harmless. Then you decided you wanted to go to Sunday school, so much to the delight of your Grandparents, Dad dropped you off at their church on Sunday morning. When Dan was old enough, you took him along as well. Dad and I attended the adult Sunday school class a couple of times but didn't find it to our liking…so we dropped out.

During the eight years after Dan was born, I became pregnant four times and lost each baby. When we realized that I was pregnant again, I went to a new doctor in town. Doctor Vander Wal was fresh out of school and eager to take the challenge. He went back to his professors for help, did lots of research, and came up with a plan. Jack, our miracle baby, was born September 20, 1955. I thanked the doctor profusely for all the extra care he had given me, and he immediately said that I wasn't to thank him for this baby…I was to thank God. Thank God? I had not thought much about God in a long time, and then I wondered…did God really care…what happened to me?

I thought seriously about coming to God on my own terms. I did not want to be involved with church…spare me the emotional stuff…I would read the Bible and hoped

that would be enough. Somehow that didn't work. The Bible was a puzzle to me, and my good intentions evaporated.

The next spring, we were under a tornado watch when I spotted a tornado in the Southwest headed in our direction. I spread the alarm, and with baby in arms, took you and Dan to the basement while Dad stayed behind to shut off the power. We sat there huddled together, waiting for the storm to hit, and I thought, "It is too late; if we die in the next few minutes, I am doomed." I felt so hopeless and lost. A few days later, I heard a lady being interviewed on the radio. She too had been in her basement with her children, and she said to them, "Just think, in the next few minutes, we may be in the arms of Jesus." My heart melted and I cried, knowing that I wanted that assurance, too; but once again, the moment passed, and I put off the decision for some other time.

We were not alone in our search for a sensible way to be a Christian. Our friends, Jack and Mary Shepard, were faced with a crisis as well. Jack's doctor, Dr Vander Wal, had told Jack that his heart was seriously damaged, and he was to go home and get his house in order. What did that mean? What did God really expect from each of us? My heart ached for Jack. I should have known how to help him. I was raised in the church, but I only knew that God was to be feared, and I was jealous of the lady who talked about being in the loving arms of Jesus.

Sometime after that, Dad, returning from a trip to New York, came upon an accident in one of the turnpike tunnels; a truck had crashed in the tunnel and was on fire. Dad listened to the driver screaming for help, but no one could get to him. Dad said, "That could have been me. I am not ready to die. We need to get back to church…we aren't doing right by the children." And that began a search for the right church.

We sold our home in Zeeland and bought a new house north of Holland. Our dream home became a nightmare. We were miserably unhappy. We missed our friends. I was pregnant again…with difficulties again. When we could, Dad took you and Dan to Ventura Church, a small Bible Church in that area. It was there that you became involved with their youth group. I was aware of your increased interest in church, but we never talked about it.

In June 1958, we hit bottom. We gave up on the new house and bought our old house back. It was good to be home again. Susie was born a few days after the move.

Once more, we studied the list of churches in our town. Jack and Mary settled on the Second Reformed Church because that pastor said God was like your buddy. Jack liked that concept. We knew better than that; God was to be feared.

We talked to Uncle Dave about the Baptist church, but they seemed quite radical to me. Then Uncle Mel and family started attending that church as well. If I remember correctly, the Baptist church was also your choice.

During the last week of October, the Baptist church held special meetings. We attended the first Sunday night, and it occurred to me that most of those people thought they were going to heaven, and I thought that was most presumptuous, but they were kind people, and we appreciated their friendliness.

Friday noon of that week, Dad came home for lunch and asked me to go to church with him that night. I said I couldn't; I had a job, working evenings. He told me he had been going every night (you babysitting, no doubt), and I thought I did not want to go on an emotional binge with him, but *I* knew that the time had come to make up my mind. After he left, I sat down at the kitchen table with the Bible, a pot of coffee, and a package of cigarettes. I asked (dared) God to show me if I was to do something as "far out" as to "get saved".

I decided it would have to be in the words of Jesus, so I searched the gospels; reading here and there, I looked for the words "get saved", but somehow, I kept stumbling onto Matthew 18: 2 &3, where Jesus said we are to come to him as little children. I knew how much I loved our children, the joy of them piling into our laps and then running off again…their unquestioning love. I suddenly understood that God wanted to love me the way I loved my children. His presence in that kitchen was so real, I knew then all I wanted, above all else, was to be His child; it was as though I had climbed into His lap. I didn't realize that I had "got saved."

We did go to church that night. At the close of the service, both Dad and I went to the prayer room. Pastor Vander Lugt prayed with me, and I wept with remorse for my sins and with joy that I was now forgiven and clean before God. He then returned to Dad and asked him where he stood. Dad, with tears in his eyes, said that on the way to Grand Rapids that afternoon, he became so overwhelmed with grief over the life he had been living, that he pulled his pick-up truck over, and there by the side of the road, asked God to forgive him.

Pastor Vander Lugt asked me if we had a Bible, and I proudly said we did. It was the Bible that Dad received when he graduated from high school. When I told him that I found it hard to understand, he gave me his Amplified New Testament Bible, which has been a good resource for me the last 51 years. Dad carried it with him in his truck for a while, which explains the binding patched with duct tape.

Lynda, I thank you for being faithful in prayer all those years, and for asking people to pray for your wicked parents. I thank God for Aunt Bertha and Ventura Church and those people who influenced you along the way. God was listening and working all the time. You were 15 when those prayers were answered, and Dad and I joined you in the family of our Heavenly Father, October 30, 1958.

When I think of all these things,
    my heart sings the Doxology
    FORTISSIMO

    Love you, Mom

Dear Sam,

It was so good to talk with you! Sounds like things are going well, and I thank God for that. You asked about Dad, and I am writing this for you only… but then maybe you can share it if you want to.

Dad was born fourth in a family of eight. His parents were very religious (Free Methodist) in a community of 95% Christian Reformed.

His father was the Railway Express agent in Zeeland, Michigan. He was a highly respected sportsman and associated with other men interested in hunting, fishing, training dogs, etc. There were a couple of doctors in that group. When they would call Grandpa and say, "Let's go fishing", Grandpa would beg off because he was in too much pain and his "Good Buddy" doctor would say, "Ach Gerrit, I can fix that" and gave him a shot of Demerol. Grandpa became addicted to Demerol. It was very sad; his last years were spent in lots of pain.

Your Grandmother was a contented, little round lady, who read her Bible, Sunday school papers, etc., and listened to soap operas on the radio every day… they were real to her. I can't remember her ever reading a book. She wasn't very bright but was a good mother. Her husband (your Grandpa) did not treat her with much respect and neither did her boys.

When Dad was eight or nine years old, he got pneumonia, which was a real killer in those days. He was in the hospital for a long time, not getting better; then they decided to drain his lungs by putting tubes in through his back. It was a desperate thing to do, but it worked. His family believed that God had saved Dad for some special work in the church and often reminded him of that. He did have a good voice, but early on, he decided not to sing solos anymore, and he began to pull back from what they thought was his calling. One time, Dad and I were laughing at Charlie Brown's dog stretched out on the top of his doghouse, saying, "There is no burden as heavy as a great potential." Dad said that was the way he felt about his parents' expectations.

Dad was very bright, and when his father developed Arthritis in the spine and neck, Dad very often helped in the Express Office. By the time he was in high school, he could run the office alone.

After Dad graduated from high school, he worked for Railway Express in Benton Harbor, and then later that year, he became the manager of the Railway Express office in Belding, Michigan.

Dad's love of cars started at the age of 13 when he decided to take his Dad's car for a ride. Fortunately, the car ran out of gas before he got too far! He bought his first car, a Model A Ford, after graduating from high school. Gas was 18 cents a gallon, and we spent many happy hours cruising around the back roads in Ottawa County, usually ending up on the shores of Lake Michigan. Dad was a happy, fun-loving guy in those days. The future was bright; the sky was the limit.

Much to his father's consternation, when your dad got away from home in Benton Harbor, he sold the Model A Ford and bought an old convertible. When he was transferred to Belding, that car had to go. It was replaced with a lumbering panel truck, which was needed to pick up and deliver express items. That vehicle was our honeymoon chariot, August 13, 1941.

Belding was a small town with a small police force.

The chief of police didn't care much for Dad's driving and became a mean bully to Dad. One day, he stopped Dad and asked for his license. He put it in his pocket and said that from then on, he was only to drive in order to work. That was no problem to Dad; he would just not be around when the train came through to pick up the day's freight, and Dad would then drive the day's freight into Grand Rapids. It got to be a game with Dad, and you can bet that Dad had more fun than that cop.

Shortly after that, Dad was drafted into the Army. He was inducted into the service in January 1943 and did his basic training at Fort Leonard Wood in Missouri. He did well in the service, got a furlough when Lynda was born in August of that year, and then in October, another furlough before he was to ship out to Europe. When he arrived back home in Michigan, he was very sick with Rheumatoid Arthritis. A local doctor contacted the Army and Dad was sent to Percy Jones Hospital in Battle Creek, Michigan. He was there until just before Christmas, when he discharged with an Honorable Medical Discharge.

Dad loved being a father; Lynda was his pride and joy. He worked different jobs, was restless, and moved on to something else. We moved several times. We bought a house south of Grand Rapids and then sold it when housing became scarce, for a lot more than what we paid for it. When Lynda was two years old, Dad accepted a job in Chicago as a dispatcher for a trucking company in Grand Rapids, Michigan. He liked the truckers but disliked being stuck in an office. He learned a lot from those truckers. In 1946, Dad bought his own truck and went to work for a furniture company, delivering furniture. We moved back to Holland, Michigan, where we lived in veteran's housing barracks, complete with pot-bellied stoves! From that time on, Dad was gone a lot. He would give up trucking, only to get restless and go back to it again.

Dan was born in 1947, and as Dan grew older, Dad carried the tradition of his father; he taught Dan how to fish and how to handle a gun. Dan became a good shot, holding his own when hunting with the Bouman Clan in the Fall hunting seasons. Jack could not sit still long enough to catch a fish or stalk a rabbit; that along with Dad's failing health put an end to most of the hunting and fishing.

In 1949, we bought the house in Zeeland, where you were born. Jack and Mary Shepard lived next door, and we were good friends until we started attending the Baptist church. We became Christians in that church, and that ended our friendship with the Shepards.

I'm kind of rambling here, and as I write, I'm thinking of the things that happened, which might have changed Dad from a happy, funny guy to a sad, disappointed man.

Dad worked hard. He learned how to improve every house we lived in. He was smart, always trying to get ahead, but he did not have the education to run with the big guys (like his Dad). It was a great disappointment to him.

Dad was 39 when you were born, wrestling with Arthritis and working for Big Dutchman. He installed automatic systems on farms, automatic chicken houses, etc. He was good at it. Big Dutchman changed their system and helped Dad start his own business. Dad was given a contract to do the same work and opened his own business. It was far too big a job for Dad. He hired people and was nice to them, only to have them cheat and steal. He did not have the management skills needed for that work and was unable to be a successful leader, another disappointment. He phased out that business shortly after we moved to Warsaw, and once more drove truck. You remember the rest.

When we became Christians, we both quit smoking. Dad couldn't stick it out, and so began the game of hiding his secret. Consequently, he was always restless, always disappearing. He loved the freedom of the open road, where he wasn't fenced in. He would come home from a trip and be so happy to see us, but every day he was home, his irritation would start building. He finally quit smoking after his heart attack, when he was working at Madison School.

I know that Dad loved you as best he could. You came along when Dad's health was failing. His dreams of success (Cage Contractors) failed, and then the heart attack that crippled him for the rest of his life. But I remember when you were working in a booth at Pike Lake. You and your friends got to fooling around (I'm sure you remember this better than I do) and the boss showed up, firing all of you. You were so upset because you were saving for a bike. Dad went to bat for you and got your job back. Then Dad bought you a bike, and I felt that it would have been better for you to learn the discipline of saving and then shopping for the bike of your choice. We argued about it, but Dad loved to give gifts, and I think he was that way because he felt bad about being gone so often and so long, and he felt that gifts would show that he loved us.

When you think of Dad, I'm sure you remember his love for cars and his skill in dickering with the salespeople until he got what he wanted. A new car for Dad was like being on a honeymoon. He was totally in love with his new toy, but after 20,000 miles or so, he would start questioning its safety, its gas mileage, etc., etc., etc., and he would start lusting after a better car, and the familiar dance would begin all over again.

Do you remember the fun we had, the games we played, and singing all kinds of songs, and making up new words for old tunes when we traveled? You have a really good voice. Do you still sing while driving? I hope so.

When I look back at our 55 years of marriage, I'm amazed at the struggles we survived. Would I have been better off marrying one of the good Christian reformed boys, who I went to high school with, living out my days in a Dutch community with a man contented with a factory job? Sounds terribly dull to me now. Life has been full of adventures, not as much security, but always hope and belief in hard work. Best of all is that without Dad, you would not be here, Sam! Or Susie, or Jack, or Dan, or Lynda. Sometimes, in the long, lonely nights,

I wrap myself in a warm, cozy blanket of good memories and just thank God for all of you. The Bible says that all things work out for good to those who love God. Is that true? Well…here I sit in a dream of a place, in a climate that loves old people, in a facility that is beautiful, and people around me, who care for me when I need help. I have survived a surgery that often kills people, but here I am, somewhat handicapped, but still playing music. Daughter-In-Law Nancy and I will be doing the dinner music in the dining room this Sunday. It is so much fun!

I love you, Sam. I'm so proud of you and pray that your days ahead will be wonderfully blessed with love and happiness.

Mom.

Dan

Zeeland, Michigan, 1965

We had five children in our family: Lynda and Dan were born four years apart; after eight years, we had a second family: Jack and Susie and Sam, with almost three years between them. It was a busy time for sure, but we worked well together, and I have many happy memories of those days.

One day, when my husband was out of town, our washer conked out, so in the evening, as I headed out the door to visit the local laundromat, Dan announced that he was now in college and needed to study and that he was too old to be helping with clean-up after dinner. That was frustration overload. I put the basket down and exhaled an exasperated, "DAMN!" Dan's eyes registered his shock. I hadn't used that word in a long time.

Here was this kid, who was so persnickety about his appearance, that he would put on a clean shirt just to run to the store. He had more than his share of stuff in that basket and now...I looked at him, and he said, "Fine" and deliberately started throwing out everything belonging to him. Finally, Dan said, "Well, umm, ok, I'll do it tonight, but that is it."

While I was loading the washers that night, I began to think that perhaps he was right. I hadn't realized that Dan's idea of a "college boy" did not include kitchen help, and maybe I was still treating him like a kid. I needed to work out some other plan. As I thought about it, I decided to teach Dan to iron his own shirts. It would be a good thing for him to know, and then too, he might be more careful about how often he changed shirts.

When I returned home with the laundry, clean and still warm from the dryers, we talked. I was sorry I had lost my temper and Dan was happy to see me in a better mood. He thought my idea was a good plan. Those were the days before permanent press, but Dan was motivated and learned quickly.

Soon after that, we were transferred to Northern Illinois. Dan lived on campus and became famous for his shirt ironing. He made some extra cash on the side from his buddies. Even to this day, Dan takes pride in ironing a good shirt, but when I'm there, I do it for him, very carefully.

Ok, Dan, that is my story. I have heard from reliable sources that you tell your version of this story to friends and that your spin gets a good howl. That's ok; we all have selective memories. I just hope your memories are as happy as mine.

Love you,

Mom

CHAPTER SIX:

Thoughts In Flight — The Poetry of Carolyn Ruth

This is about Jack. Every storm for Suz found
her at the window cheering God on.

SUMMMER STORM

By Carolyn Baker

Out of the night comes a far-off rumble
A toddler bounds to his mother's side
It was fun to count between flash and thunder
No danger here where we safely hide
But nature staged a grand finale
Elements colliding with a resounding crash
And a little voice squeaks
"Can I get in the middle?"
With laughter we cuddle him between us
And store up the memory for our Golden Years

Dust Devil
Hey! You dizzy dust devil
Twirling in the sun.
Do you think
You are the only one
Having any fun?
Well! I'll dance to my music
And you can dance to yours
Just stay away from my house
When I'm out of doors.

Carolyn Baker 05-24-2004

These are my genes, inherited!
This is the way I am
But a voice within me, struggling to be heard, says
"You invited me in and that is not the way I am."

I probably sent you this before, changed it many times. Most recent fix.

Oh build me a shelter of words true and tested
Encouraging words to stay the course
Gracious words for those needing rest
Worthy words to build strength and endurance
And truthful words keeping God in focus

Now in the evening when all is still
Thoughts drifting here and there
Living words flash upon my inward eye
And then my heart with wonder fills
As words found and memorized so long ago
Surface as needed, delighting my soul

Wonderful words of life

Chess Pieces

I am a Pawn
I was born a Pawn
My dad loved me
He was a Pawn too
Struggling through life
On another person's board

I married an aspiring King
I dreamed of being a Queen
And sometimes I was
But usually plodded on
In my pawnly ways
On another person's board

We had five Pawns
To train for higher service
Sometimes they were Knights
And sometimes they were not
Pawnishness is hard to shake
On another person's board

The playing field is thinning
I am a pawn of circumstances
With fewer options
Aimless, yet searching
On this my lonesome board

Another king beckons me
To be a Rook, or Knight, or Bishop?
I think not!
(I revel in good pawnmanship)
On this my chosen board

This one thing I know:
When the battles are over,
When I reach that far side
I will be one happy Pawn
On my master's board
Carolyn Baker, January 1, 1998

I wrote this one when I was getting ready to visit Lynda in Iceland.

> You say you will miss me
> I'm sure you will
> But not for love engendered
> You say you will miss me
> You can bet on that
> For loss of services rendered

Now, looking back, I should have stayed home. I missed you guys!

And that is the way it goes…you plow through life, making decisions left and right and all over the place. Some good, some bad, some unimportant, and some life changing, but at that time you can't know which is which. I am sure thankful for Romans 8:28.

Love to all,

Mom

Worship by Carolyn Baker @ carolynruth@copper.net

I worship you, Lord
When the day is bright.
The earth is in its splendor
I enjoy with delight.
The gift of days beyond three and ten
Are cherished each day
Again and again.

I worship you, Lord
In the great congregation,
When music swells
In great adoration.
I echo the artistry
Of composer and pen.
And join in your praise
With a fervent "Amen."

I worship you, Lord
When in deep trouble.
You prune my ways of wood hay and stubble.
Your spirit leads to a higher path.
Your word abides as rod and staff.

I worship you, Lord, when full of years,
Staggered by loss, nagged by fears.
I bow beneath your mighty hand (I Peter 5:6)
Not seeing, yet believing that your plan
Is blessing of the highest degree.
My Lord and my God, I worship Thee.

ALLERGIES

Anonymous

I have an incontinent nose
Like a faucet it drips and it flows
I've petitioned Depends
For a product that ends
The drip from my lip to my toes

January 2004
Oh the struggle
Of a cold gone bad
Resident in bronchi
And phlegm filled head
Together we sail
This hacking sea
Til I get rid of it
Or it gets rid of me.

FREEDOM

All the sins that I've committed
All the wrongs that I have done
Hateful, selfish, mean, and hurtful
All exposed beneath the sun

God forgives them all
God forgives them all
All the sins that I've committed
God forgives them all

All the hurts that I have suffered
All the losses great and small
All the shattered expectations
Aged and yellow on my wall

I forgive them all
I forgive them all
God forgave me, I forgive you
I forgive them all

I sing this to the tune of "I Surrender All" as many
times as necessary.
Mom

WORDS – November Storm
Words, words everywhere
Flying wildly through the air
Like galloping verbosity.
Words, words everywhere,
This must be leap year.
Harsh karate words threatening disaster,
Ominous words playing on our fears.
lovely words, encouraging words,
Promising a perfect here-after.
Roman candle words that thrill then fade away.
Cotton candy philosophies spinning lofty dreams,
Oh, don't we wish it could be as good as it seems;
Inspirational words, two or three in a row,
Coining clever slogans, it happens every four.
But now the day is over, it is time to put to rest
The driving storm of pounding words,
Tomorrow is the test.

Out of the night the workers move
To their appointed places.
Into the day the voters surge,
With two words left in play
Is it "Yea"? or is it "Nay"?
All day long and into the night
The tally rambles from left to right
With tense expectation the country waits
And cautious commentators also wait,
(Having learned from Kaltenborn)
Every precinct must be heard from,
To this right we are born.

Kaltenborn: Google 1948 presidential election Dewey vs Truman.

Written after Obama's election, 2008

If by some power the gift were given
To see ourselves as seen from heaven
God spares us the terror of being exposed
For His Grace is weaving our heavenly clothes

Isaiah 61:10
C.R. Baker

At last, at last the blizzard ends,
Some rejoice and others lament.
Tattered banners and millions of signs
Go down in history, a new day begins.
The future is a guessing game
Tilted by the strengths and foibles of men
Yet may our words be few but clear
Echoing from our forefathers true and just,
In God --- oh yes,
IN GOD WE TRUST

Carolyn Bouman Baker 10-2008

WORDS OF LIFE
By Carolyn Baker

Words that bubble my heart to laughter
Pretty words flowing with lighthearted banter

Words working together on a Sunday afternoon
Like melted chocolate on vanilla ice cream

Rigid words in perfect order
Marching lock-step down the page

Energized words with bombastic salvos
Daring a conquest of lurking shadows

But then I wake from my dreamy state

And life is rough

Fly away my pretty words
I'm in need of sturdier stuff

Words plain and simple
That get to the point

Words that address the aching joint,
The blurry eyes, the fallen arches,
Ebbing energy before day's end and
Repeated irritants stressing my soul

SECURITY

July 1996

When sorry descends like the sky is falling
When all loving help still leaves you alone,
Be still and know, it is God's voice calling
I AM your refuge, come home, come home.

July 2001

When troubles mount like roaring breakers,
When all who would help are asleep in their homes
Be quiet, listen, it is God's voice whispering
I AM here…you are not alone.

C.R. Baker

Spring 1970

When shaking out rugs you scold the breeze
That is trying to tell you of newly dressed trees.
Scrub if you will, polish and scour
toiling never made even one little flower.

Be still and listen, look up and behold,
For God has created perfection untold.
So, why not?
Kick off your shoes, toes deep in grass
Hurry! It's Spring flying past.

Dedicated dirt chaser doing your thing.
That's not the way to celebrate spring.
With a swish and a bang you banish the dust.
Clouding the issue with all your fuss.

THE WIND

By Carolyn Baker

Swishing, swooshing
Ducking and weaving
Like a frenzied conductor
Who has lost his marbles
So blows the winter wind

EARLY FLIGHT

By Carolyn Baker

Here I lay upon my bed looking at the ceiling. I've told myself to go to sleep, but my mind isn't willing. I have prayed for kinfolk near and far, asking God to bless them.

I've checked the alarm clock to be sure it would ring AM, not PM! Now, that would be a fright. I've double checked the luggage, complete with something to read and something to eat.

Be quiet, mind! Go to sleep.

Memory drifts lazily into other days, children: their school years, basketball and plays, struggles and victories, sometimes long in coming. Birthday parties with grandparents and friends. Holidays, vacations, recitals, and graduations all gathered, sweet and mellow, in the wee, small hours of the night.

My favorite music comes bouncing through my head…am I dreaming? No, I'm wide awake, tapping the temp on my pillow.

I've counted backwards from one hundred by seven to be sure the Alzheimer Boogie Man isn't coming around the bend.

In just one hour, the alarm will ring, but not to fear, I can sleep on the plane. In one hour! Do you suppose I will hear the bell? Or will I, at last,……. be………. sleeping.

The Wind and I

I love the wind…the feel of it, the smell of it, the taste of it, the sound of it. Where does the wind come from? Did someone sneeze in China last week, starting a chain reaction? The wind is a mystery, invisible, yet evident everywhere.

I laugh with the wind in a frisky mood, tossing branches and swirling leaves with capricious abandonment, and I chuckle at the winds that taunt and tease empty sails on a becalmed sea.

I thrill to the sight of the wind toying with our country's flag, flapping and reaching with snappy salutes for the world to see…. By God's grace, we are still here, we are still free.

I brace myself in the dead of winter, when the winds, howling and screeching, whistle through invisible cracks; and those awesome Grandfather winds that moan and groan in the bass cleft, while the Grandmother winds emote, keening in high C, "Why meeee, why meeeee?"

Sometimes on a cold winter's night, I feel like I'm spying when I watch the winds dancing with naked trees, all swirling in black and white while nature's music undulates in a minor key. I welcome the winds that treat us to the aroma of rain kissed Creosote bushes in the Arizona desert or the delicate scent of Eucalyptus trees on the wind-whipped Pacific coasts of California.

I shiver with delight at the first tiny breeze at the end of a long sultry day, inhaling with gratitude until my lungs almost burst.

I am leery of winds that roll the clouds, spiraling, twisting and turning; those winds send the wise and prudent to their basements until the angst of nature passes by. Then, with the impulsiveness of a two-year old child, that same wind gentles down to stage an armada of fleecy clouds, playing "Hide and Go Seek" with the moon as they sail through the night.

I forgive the winds that hassle my hair and water my eyes…that sometimes promises rain and often tells me lies…and oh, those tricky autumn winds that strip the trees of burnished leaves…I can almost hear them sing, "Free at last, free at last", as they meander down the mud puddle below.

I applaud the boisterous Northwest winds on a stormy, November day that drive with mighty determination the sagging clouds and swelling waves down the full length of Lake Michigan; pushing, building, faster and higher, exploding with tremendous energy as they sideswipe breakwaters, piers, and lighthouses along the way. It is like watching gigantic waves in a gigantic teacup sloshing with reckless glee until it splashes all over its southern shore without so much as a "Pardon me."

I marvel at the power of the monster storms; hurricanes, tornadoes, and blizzards; winds that create stories of rampant devastation, terrible losses, mighty heroes, and miraculous survivors. Stories to be told again and again; milestones marking time and place in our personal histories.

As I face into the wind, my narcissistic eye often catches reflections of my own shifting moods and there I find a kindred spirit; sometimes happy, sometimes sad, sometimes spirited, sometimes dull, sometimes gentle, sometimes rough, rarely foe, more often friend. As I love myself, I love the wind.

By Carolyn Baker

February 2008

Hope this doesn't blow you away.

Love,

Mom

If I could harness my thoughts in flight
Metered and rhymed and set just right
What a fantastic poet I would be
Polished and published for all to see!
Imagine that.

C.R.B.

The End.

APPENDIX:

In Her Own Hand: A Selection of Carolyn's Handwritten Pages

(Checkmarks and some notes belong to the teacher of a writing class.)

In Michigan

Every Spring as a child I remember
The return of the birds – the compitition
to see the first Robin, The first blueBird
the first red winged black bird – *

*
Cardinals
Bluejays
hummers

All Winter Long we had faithfully
fed The Sparrows and The return of
~~tf~~ and the ~~bright flashs~~ Colors of
The Summer population always meant
The cold sluggist Winter was over and
the ~~foretelling~~ The Bright Colors of the
birds soon Would be duplicated ~~within~~ in
the ~~spring flowers~~ arrival of flowers
deep in the woods ~~gardens~~ Waiting for
our hike To gather.

Syrup in a Can
ash Trays

295 4431
Norma Walker

let the water
do not run the ~~water~~ while
brushing teeth

Depression years - house full
of people. wasting water in
small amounts helped the water bill
— once mentioned to friends + they
laughed at such a thing — now
Think green — it is on the list
along with 'small continuous drips
waste huge amounts of water etc

viewing small things — consistently repeated
have a great influence —

Article "How To be a millionair

APRIL 16 ✓

Easter when I was a child, was purely religious in our home. I remember the sunrise services and the feeling of joy in the air. Yes - there were bunnies & chocolate eggs. but not in our home My father in law always gave my mother in law a always large chocolate egg on Easter. I commented - often to my husband how nice that was - how kind & thoughtful but I never received a chocolate egg. My husband loved or giving me just the right gift for other occasions. But to this day I have yet to receive a chocolate egg.

Amy think about spring may 7th 9 a.m.

✓ You say you will miss me?

December 2, 09

I have kept *cherished* Memories for all these years because they bring to mind the good things that happened during a rough and difficult time in my life

I was the 6th child (4th daughter) in a large family but an older sister became our chief leader — bringing happy times — almost out of nothing —
Christmas 1932 — no tree — Marian arranged boxes to form a fake fireplace — covered it with paper with a red brick pattern — went out to the woods for pieces of wood — using red paper to imitate a fire — when viewed through half closed eyes — we could almost believe it was real

1932!?! No money! Not to fear, Marian helped us make gifts — pin cushions from scraps of cloth — vases from discarded jars covered with envelope liners from last years cards — then varnished — we had piles of small gifts — some of them our own *given* toys — the gifts

I can still see my *persons* mother laughing over still another pot holder.

Blanch
DORIS

May 2? 09 ✓

Camping at Ottowa Beach:

Eating Lund one June day I remembered my H.s days when my school friends took the 1st wk. of vacation camping at O.B. — but my mother wouldn't let me do that - to much hanky panky etc.

I mentioned it to Gordon and he said - lets go — in one hour we were on our way— 2 hours drive and we were setting up a borrowed Tent and we just inhaled deeply of the lake Michigan air, the aroma of the ~~the lake~~ the bliss of being again at the playground of our dating days was wonderful - and then we realized that two retired people were dead center in a mob of teenagers - wondered if we would get any sleep - But we did — the rules were strictly enforced and we felt like we were young again

the next day we teded up our camp and left to see friends + family

While we were gone a storm came up which blew down our tent & soaked all our belongings - we spent 2 hours cleaning up - packed the car - headed for Rosi's and checked into a motel

Finish this on summer Vacation 6-24

For Horizons.

Next meeting 4-13   3-23 —

What did I do this week that just made me laugh —

✓ I read a really tempting receipe so —
I got assembled all the ingredients lined up —
— easy recipe — Put it in the oven
and then my neighbor to come and
cretique this delicious dessert —
Well — it fell 190 pts below my
expectations — what was there to do
but num nibble and squint — —
we had fun though — The storm sent
her scurrying for home and I sat by
Cand The power cut off so I thought
good I'll just cuddle up and watch
T.V. by candle light. Right!

Pray for Gwen — daughter of Joan O'Bert.

Possible M.S.

Next
Mar 9 — 23

✓ 2-16-07

(Widowed)

this Valentines day I said "Grow up"
The past is past — But forgot To Tell my
friends — Received Cards and calls from
family — from Lynda who was snowed-in
happy as clam for the break — Rox had
us "girls" over for a wonderful lunch and
To celibrate my marriage to Tim anniversary
and I felt loved + contended in my
"pleasant pastures". (#9 years)

✓   10-6-06

This year I want to be more disciplined
with my time To determin what needs to
be done and Then stay focused. It's LIKE
I'm fighting a Tide that is carryind my
hours away with very little To show for it.
I need To prioritize and not imatate
Snoopy who Lays on Top of his dog house
Saying " LEARN FROM THE PAST, PLAN
FOR THE FUTURE — RESt This AFTERNOON "

8-24-06

If somebody wanted to buy me for a gift for my your Collection what would you like for you a ?

a Ceramic Pilated Wood pecker in Memory of seeing that beautiful, statuesque statuesque bird out of Dan's Kitchen Window - deep in The Woods of British Columbia - it would be an impressive addition to my bird Collection of 3

1987

My daughter Susie and her husband Mark are Avid Sailors so the decor in their home is Nautical - They Collect Lighthouses and will Travel miles out of the way to visit Light them in person

Mark is a composer, has written a piece called "Barque So frail" about a small Sail boat in a storm

So me They have visited many of The Lighthouses in their collection

Quickies   7-28-06

This week I saw new opportunities
in friendships at 7. H.E. My prayer is   TO HER.
that I may be of help and encouragement.
I'm more keenly aware of the brevity
of our lives due to the sudden loss of
Pauline Brooks with a massive stroke.
And This new friend — God help me

Forth of July at Far Horizons East.

A Large percent of the men living at 7H.E.
served in the II World War. I had forgotten
what old fashioned Patriotism was Like until
I watched this group put together a 4th of July
~~parade along with energy Like decorations~~
First order of the day was gathering
around The flag pole ~~and it~~ as the flag
was raised and the salute — Then the
parade — home made floats, decorated Cars
and the men — serious, reverent, marching
in their uniforms — Pride in every step

This was followed by a breakfast of sausage
and egg Sandwiches, fruit and Coffee —

A Program followed with a reading about
the development of our flag ~~The battles~~
The history of its changes — read by a ~~the~~
grown ~~man~~ who Could hardly keep his
emotions under Control

these were The men who had put
their lives on the line for their Country
who signed up right after Pearl
hardor — who fought with conviction and
watches their buddys die - To them —
our Country was loved with action
and commitment. We are all one
cohesive unit - The unite States of America

Quicky's   6-16-08

Favorite pass Time as a child was reading.
With so many siblings it was my escape
To other worlds. There was a bookcase.
Next To a recliner in one corner — the
space in the corner was my hide all away
— my mother hid her mending in a box
back there and it was my throne — As soon
as I was old enough To walk alone To the
library my corner was always there for
me with the latest book

    When parents died we could name what
we wanted out of the house — all I wanted
was the bookcase — Crafted by my paternal
grandfather — The next trip to canada we
took it to Dan — who is also an excellent
cabinet maker — to be sure the bookcase
stayed in the family

Changes — 17 years in Warsaw, 15 years with
Win-Some Women (closer then family) leaving
behind our little house, with large windows showing Trees, birds,
playful squirrels — my pleasure in watching
the wild life in the changing season.
    The furniture van left — we were all packed
E.T.D. — after the closing session on my last
retreat —
    And where were we going? To The desert
visions of sitting on a sand pile in the middle
of nowhere.
    God had plans for us beyond my wildest
dreams. The modular home we had purchased
in Tucson needed.

Community
orchestra

V   2-9-06

My Mom could rule the world but my Dad took care of the money - Every week he would get out his box of envelopes ON PAY DAY, Carefully marked - divid his pay check 2.00 s here - 5.00 there. ☒ Once in the envelope it *never* was withdrawn for any other purpose than stated on that envelope. I never heard any arguements or discussions about money. I know my mons had cash for groceries & the frequent peddlers but in our ~~home was~~ considering the size of our family and the meger years ~~never I never~~ ~~heard an argeement about money - Dad~~ ~~did a good job.~~

Early 'Dave Ramsey' style!
SK

This week when I saw the snow on the mountains I remembered the winters in michigan we lived in an area with gentle hills and we spent lots of time sledding, skiing - we making Fox and Geese patterss for playing. Tic and snow forts fortified with lots of snow balls for we didn't have snow suits in my day but we layered on extra clothing and when we were soaked through we would come in and hang the clothes to dry - Then as soon as they were dry we would go out and to it all over again.

2-27-00 ✓

When I think of the rodeo I remember all the Zane Grey Novels I devoured as a child – The wild wild West Was a far country from Holland Michigan but In my dreams I Lived it.

When we made our 1st Cross Countr Trip to Vancouver, B.C We had a CB radio in The Car. As we passed Through the West – The DK's Wyoming, Idah – Some one on the C.B. gave us the story of Custers Last Stand. It was on That hill that This happened – It was over there that — I felt Like I was living it in person :

2-10-06

When I picture a garden I think of my
Dad — quite, hard working and a gift for
raising the best garden in the world. He
would ride his bike to work in the mornin
go from there to a rich plot of ground —
in th afternoon and work the garden
with love and skill — he would come
rideing in deering the evening loaded
with fresh vegies — having stopped on
the way home to share with his sesta
and some other friends along the way
It was his life long hobby— He
spadded over the rich river muck on his
plot by hand and his gentle soul was
nourished as well as all those who
receieved from his bounty

2-4-06

~~Choose an event~~

One of my favorite toys was roller skates. It granted me the freedom of the streets. Our part of town had gentle hills and I can still feel the exhileration of flying down the hill coasting to a stop and then puffing up the hill to do it all again. Spring was so long in coming to Holland Michigan so when the weather started warming up we appreciated it doubly. We had the run of the town and roller skates was my favorite way of seeing it all.

Worn out wheels, lost skate keys & Hot Weather usual brought it to an end.

"my best memory of camp is when we decided to chuck everything and head out to Ottowa Beach, Holland Michigan — my old stamping grounds — when I was in H.S. many of my friends spent the 1st week of summer camping. But MY mom wouldn't let me. So those days in June always made me feel deprived — So — Gordon & I threw a bunch of things in the car and headed out 125 mile away.

We pitched our tent late in the afternoon and soon realized we were in the middle of a mob of teenagers ready to party — the tradition had survive It was fun to be a spectator

I mentioned this to Gordon one noon

✓

10-28-08

Road Trip

First ~~trip~~ First trip to Vancouver —

Dan had left for Canada in 1971 — We had
not seen him for 5 years. In aug 1976
We decided to make the long trek in
a new Aspen (dodge) — We had 10 days.
We arranged mattresses in the ~~back~~ packed
some food and set out from Warsaw — I had
never been west of Kansas City — Had read
every Zane Grey ever written and now we
were at last going to see the West. We
stayed motels on alternate nights — ate one
big meal in a resturant per day — every
mile bringing us Closer to our first son.
It was "wonderful" the C.B. radio kept us
entertained — listening to other travelers. talking
about the history of the places we passed —
We left Warsaw on Frid p.m. arrived in Van.
Monday night — what a reunion

Follow up on Camping/road Trip etc

First day of school as a child.

I was 4 years old - ~~almost 5~~ walked to school with
my sisters - ~~who were~~ I was a little shy
but ~~knew I had~~ sister accostomed to being
with a group - my sisters were in the 2nd -
4th & 6th grade - kindergarden required
~~idea~~ to write your first name, Tie your own
shoe laces and know the colors.
The Night before, I Sat at the diningroom with
Table and wrote my name - Cursive - with ~~my~~ my
~~Dad watching I was~~ ready
He pronounced me _____ ?

School story Next Week 10·28

✓ 10·7·05

when
I think of Sunday afternoons in the
Summer. I ~~always~~ 6 or 7 years old. ~~and~~
My Dad asked who would like to go for a
walk — I ~~was the only volunteer~~ ~~so off we went~~, just the two of us.
Every block or so he would change sides so
my arm wouldn't get tired. He told me
about the tradition — men walking on the
street side when for a walk with a lady
to protect her from the traffic in the
streets.

Walking with my Dad always ended up
at the railroad track — this particular
sunday we picked wild strawberries
along side ~~the Railroad~~ tracks — talking ~~some~~ saw
some but just enjoying the after~~noon~~ I knew
we would putter around there until a
train came by. My Dad was fascinated with
trains. He was an amature photographer —
Complete with a tripod, camera and a black clothe ~~thrown~~
throw over his head. He loved to photgraph
trains. Was known to have hiked 5 miles up
the track to get pictures of a train wreck

Eventualy the train came — didn't slow up
much for our little town.

then slowly we made our way back home again —
passing houses with good Dutch people
rocking away on their front porch — exchanga
greetings + ~~pleasantries~~. everyone liked my
sweet gentle Dad
I get pleasantly drowsy just thinking about
those ~~things~~ days — like a really good dream that
somehow flew away

✓   10-4

Banana Bread

When I eat ~~blank~~ I always remember
our rare trips to Getz Farm - on Lake Mich.
my dad ^{drove} the Model T the back 2 deep in
kids - The youngest on my moms Lap -
We would pack a lunch and head out
to this fabulous place on the Lake -
my first ex~~perience with~~ ^{memory of} a zoo - We
needed to go back out to the Car to
eat - Not allowed inside the zoo area -
I close my eyes and can see us gathered
around eating that wonderful banana bread -
- it is the ^{same} recipe I use to this day.

me too! sk

Bring recipe for Banana Bread

any thing to do with food

153

9-30-05   ✓   "CRASH" DVD

This I SAW ^(rather), heard a rasping noise outside
my Kitchen Window - thought is was the Lawn
man but the Noise persisted - finally I put
my work aside and investigated - ^(by my Kitchen)
There ^(I saw) on a lower branch in the tree was ^(with)
a large bird - speckled breast - a hawks bill
opening & closing his mouth at intervals
- Sounding like he ^(severe) harigitis - its Tail was not
tapered but Like it had been squared -
with that much To go on I searched my
old faith^(u) birding book and decided it was.
a Cooper's hawk, I've never been that close to
a   6   ''   before

Class

What fun things do you want people to know about you

1. I'm a recovering practical joker
2. I love to hear people laugh
3. I appreciate a good joke

Finish these sentences

1. When I think of trees I remember my toddler years and the cotton woods in the side yard. What were they saying as they whispered in the night? Were they telling secrets? Were they saying "Don't touch me"? or "Come closer"? Whatever; I'm sure it was nice.

2. I Hit him with a flip of my hand, coy and flirty - how else would a nice girl respond? Later, he wrote "__ (Sunday night in church)
"Sweetness was her nature,
~~Sharpness~~ snappy was her creed,
But the first time I attempted
I found her hand had speed."

3. The clouds were white and billowy as we drove endless miles across the mid west; three kids in the back seat of a Volkswagon. We pretended the Were castles or ski runs or high ocean waves. We took turns telling stories about what we imagined in the sky

Nov. 29, 01   For Hong Widow

I Cor 4:7-18

After listing the pressure points in my life right now, I needed to write ——

Dear Lord Jesus,

Well, here I am, Lord, 79 years old — older than I ever expected to be, with a passion and a purpose for being here. Forgive me for even mentioning the side effects of aging. When I view my life through your eyes, I feel like a child, crying because the IceCream cone is gone. Help me to see with your eyes, to seek out your mind, that as I lose physical strengths I may gain spiritual aguity — to reflect you in all things

Thank you

I Love you

Good night

Love Trib !

pg 1 seems to be missing... ✓

has perfected the plan to Hijack planes, to fly them, Loaded into crowded buildings, Dear Father comfort the Wives + hubands + children left behind. Open their hearts and minds to your word, I weep for them in their grief. I pray also for this Country, for President Bush, for those who are working in the disaster areas, give them strength and skill for the awesome task ahead.

Psalm 103:15-17

As for man, his days are like grass;
as a flower of the field, so he flourishes.
For the wind blows over it, and it is gone,
And it's place remembers it no more
But the mercy of the Lord is from everlasting
to everlasting, ON THOSE WHO FEAR HIM.

The brevity of Life is an expression of grace for those who hope in Jesus Christ. (Walter Henrichsen)

Sept. 18, 01

Psalm 77 | VS. 1-8 Complaining To God in dispare-have you forgotten me? VS 10 And I said "THis is MY ANGUISH, but I will remember the years of the right hand of the most high God." I will remember how He Sought me out, how He made me hungry for Him. How He crafted circumstances, people and my desperate needs to prepare me - to nullify my clever reasonings - to bring me to complete dissatisfaction, with myself and longing for peace with Him. I remember how God opened my eyes that fall after noon when I went to His word and dared Him to show me that I should do something so far out as "GET SAVED" I wanted God but was

scared to death of the "church" and all it's
Trappings. The hemoganized minds, the social
restrictions, the politics, conforming the members
to an indistinct simalarity. My mind cried " God
made me _ ME - not a copy of thee !"
BUT GOD said in Matt 18 Come to me _ Like Jack
and Susie Come to you. I want to Love you Just
the way you Love them. I want to take Care of
you _ enjoy you _ and you enjoy me. I Want to
teach you my ways, share with you my secrets".
And I felt as though God's very arms were
around me, flooding me with His Love. In verse 8
of Matt 18 He also said, " I know what goes on
in THE CHURCH, but don't worry about it, I will
take care of it. And I cuddled close to Him and
didn't know that I had gotten "SAVED"

Yes Lord I remember those early days, how
you had this wonderful little church with a
caring pastor, always ready to explore my
immature questions, helpful but no dictarial, Torial
kind and gentle. I remember Lord, how you
brought a friend into my Life who was in Love
with your Word, how she shared her enthusiasm
with and encourged me by example to
memorize the scriptures. And I ate your Words
in memorization and yours words beame
unto me the joy and rejoicing of my heart"
"Your way is in the Sanctuary of your Word !
Who is so great as our God?"
You changed me from a frightened young mother
and wife to a confident, "full of years" women.
Please continue to guide my ways. Help me

Jer. 15:16
Psalm 77: 13

158

to be quiet so that I may hear your voice
and some of the goodness that you have
given to me will be shared with those
you have put into my life.
And now, as I leave the horrors of last week
in your hands I deliberately <u>remember</u> who you
are and that you are my Father I need nought else
beside, for "Who is so great as our God" / Psalm 77:13

Thoughts on forgiveness —
Eph 4:32 Be kind and compassionate to one another,
forgiving eachother, just as in Christ God
forgave you.
Psalm 32:5 Then I acknowledged my sin to you
and did not cover up my iniquity,
I said "I will confess my transgressions to
the Lord"—
And you forgave the guilt of my sin
Luke 23:34 Jesus said "Father forgive them, for they do not
know what they are doing"
John 20:22,23 "Receive the Holy Spirit (Eph. 1:13B Having
believed, you were marked in Him with a seal, the
promised Holy Spirit.) vs. 23 "If you forgive anyone
his sins, they are forgiven; if you do not forgive
them, they are not forgiven"

1-13-

One special thing I did this Christmas was find Time at my daughters house to just enjoy people -- the Little bodies flying arou the ear splitter screaches - just one decible shat of Rock music - the joy of Watching a Toddler explore his universe - all Conversations carryed on above the joyful clatter - I didn't fix a single meal or any clean up - Age has its perks
that was a first

"IT's easy To be brave from a safe distance"

1985- With no bookeeping experience I accepted the position of office manager for "Win-some Wor Winona Lake, IN. I received all materials and instructions from previous manager who wa also private secretary to president of a college I was overwhelmed- So much of the work was redundlent - sending unnecessary Corespador - poor accounting etc. etc.
When The reservations started pouring in for the Next retreat I didn't have a clue as to how I would keep track of 4 different plans 3 different housing places - I needed To chuck every thing I'd been told and simplify to something I Could Visulize

✓

(Christmas)   Dec. 58 Zeeland

Discribe the Christmas that has been the

most meaningful To you –

Christmas 1958

Lynda 15, Dan, 11, Jack 3, Susie 5 mo.

Gordon & I had become believers on

Holoween night that year – 3 weeks later

Gordon has an appendectomy – no work

for 6 weeks – no income.

Christmas just around the Corner – of

course both our familys were in the

area and helped us but what to do

for gifts? We bought canning wax

and had fun making candles as gifts

to our extended families –

Gods first big lesson to us was to

swallow or pride and except help

John Templeton

An attitude of gratitude create blessing.
1955

Every year for Christmas we would always
get carried away — always we determined
to stay on budget — always we charged
stuff — so — one year I joined the Christmas
Club at our bank — didn't tell a soul — on
Dec. 1 my check arrived and I prodely
presented it to my husband. — Now did that
stop the charging — no way — we just had
a wonderful Christmas where wishs did come
true.

Dan — 3 year old — rejecting Santa Claus

1950's Zeeland Mich.

Every fall our family would- go phesant hunting in Ottowa County Michigan. Opening day found the farm roads crowded with out of the area hunters eager to get a shot at the ~~over pheasants population~~ phesant ~~numerous~~ & bountiful crop of phesants in our County.

During the season (3 wks.) we would often pack the children in the back seat of the ~~car~~ station wagon and off we'd go — road hunting — all of us scanning, searching for that well defined head of the ring necked pheasant - the guns ~~were loaded~~ ready to go — toward dusk was the best time — It was a fun family time — My husband was an excellent shot - ~~Common~~ from a family ~~with~~ son & his father a father who taught his boys well ~~the~~ good sportsman & safety in the sports world

perch fishing

Look at fall traditeous } anything continued
in your family } or passed on

1957 ✓

My first love was art DeFouw — we met at a youth for Christ meeting - I was 15 and he 18 — I played violin at, I had black hair, I wore a red ribbon in my hair — He was smitten. He was tall, blond and very serious, Most of our dates were church related or the just hanging at my house playing games with my family

His mother died, I didn't see him for a few weeks — it was over ~~he finish H.S.~~ ~~touth~~ I was young & frivolous he was older and serious — Later He became a minister in the Methodist church- Married had 4 Kids Was wounded in the war - died young. — My sweet good looking gentle ART

gave my first Valentine — choc covered cherries

Weslyan Church 1936 — Pastors wife
Lovely Lady Conducted Contata's
for Easter — at last I was old enough
to envolved in adult? activities

Mrs. Merideth was an accomplished
musician and could charm the lowest
of us into perfection — all of my family
did a lot of singing together but this
music was a lot more advanced than
the simple hymns and choroses.
    We worked hard — this was a small
Church — small choir but — the perfection
required from each of us was pure joy

Darline Cowden

165

Private Nurse
"Miss Gilroy"   Spring of 1929

Scarlet Fever (Florence)   1st grade
Quarenteen sign on door
Dad slept in the basement — so
could go to work.
Wood stove in kitchen
~~Had~~ slip on bricks in folks B.R. joyfeous
Steely Played joke on Nurse pretending to
be stuck in ~~space~~ THE CORNER SPACE between tub & wall.
She fell for it — was angry when we
all (7 kids) laughed — Mom scolded &
laughed at the same time —
I ran a slight fever one day of
the Quarenteen — spent the day
by myself in the corner behind
the wood cook stove in kitchen —
Miss Skertchy (city health nurse)
said I probably had a slight case
of scarlet fever & would be immune
— ~~Og~~ Harriet, Marion, Florence &
I — walked down river ave to the
City health Dept. to be examined before
being readmitted to school — (1st grade)
Our house was also fumigated by
the City health dept. before sign
could be taken down

I think mom was pregnant — that's why
Florence had to have a private nurse

✓ ①

When I drive the busy streets of Tusson I marvel at the collective skill of the thousands of drivers on our streets racing to & fro, and for the most part safely.

I think back ~~four~~ score years or ~~so~~ ago – To the beginning of America's great romance with Automobils – then ofter refered to as "machines" I remember our first car, ~~I was 7 or 8 years old at the time~~. A Ford model T. It had a few miles on it but everyone persuaded Dad that he could easily learn To drive. Now – a "model T" was not an easy car to master. The first challenge was to get it started. Sometimes the machine needed to be cranked. A special tool, called a crank, was inserted somewher behind the front bumped and turned quickly to start the motor. If this was done carelessly the crank could spin around and break an arm – just like that!

My Dad had zero experience with motors or machines. He was a bike man, but he was game So with an experiened friend along to help him he backed out of the drive way, fiddling with the shift – meshing the gears just so and after a few jerky lurches he was on his way. We all watche him go – praying for his safety

167

(2)

I have been driving for 59 years. I earned my first Ticket in 1996 — for ~~for~~ presuming on the grace of a yellow light. ~~I Took the drivers Training~~ at Speedway & Ko16.
I attended The Drivers Training class and it was well worth The cost.
I Thank God for The many miles of Safe driving — Times that I Could have been Tickited and Times when I was spared in close calls. I am Thankful ~~For now Im~~ I'm so Thankful

what was the first movie I saw

In the Traditions of my Solid Dutch family
movies were Verboten, but on This
Thanksgiving Day 1938 our huge dinner
over — the kitchen all spiffed up the
older children — 11-21 decided
To go for a ride — somewhere along
The way we decided To see a movie —
— we drove To Grand Rapids (25 miles)
To See Lady of The Tropics — what an
eye opener — the Tropics, so far removed
from cold michigan — The Beautiful
women — The threatening men

Favorite Movie Today — The seduction of Doctor
Lewis ___

Opens with a veew of the laid off workers
picking up their welfare checks — The plan was
to Lure a factory To their Island — but no Doctor
on Island — no factory — They advertize
and receive an applicant —

Pat | American PResident "Laura"

DR. Chifago

AFRican Queen
Casablaca

Childhood ✓

My childhood hero —
HER NAME WAS MYRTLE ~~Deaton~~ GREEN. I was in
the third grade. She was my S.S. Teacher —
She was beautiful, smelled of perfume —
Spoke softly and always kind.

I knew for sure she loved me.
I just knew.

She had our class over for a party.
Every thing was perfect — she served
a dessert out of Better Homes & Gardens
½ half banana ☐ upright in a pineapple
Ring with cherry on top. I didn't know
how to eat it but we watched her — whew
She was a wonderful lady — maybe 25

Our big adventure was to drive to Zeeland,
5 miles to the east. Dad decided to take a
less traveled ~~route~~ ~~which~~ but it had one
problem — approaching Zeeland from the
South presented a steep short hill. ~~We were~~
6 of us ~~decked 2 deep in the back seat.~~ Before we
started up the hill dad told us that if the
car stalled we were to get out quickly on the
right hand side. ~~You~~ I remember the
ridged tension and the united sigh of
relief as we made it to the Top.

We had a light hearted drive back To
Holland. ~~We stopped~~ at a gas station that was
Celebrating their ~~new~~ grand opening with Candy
Bars for adults and balloons for children.
When Dad paid his bill — They asked how many
children and my Dad said 7 — They said
" No way" Came out To Check — Sure enough
one on Mom's lap in the front and six of us
double deckered in The back Seat.

I was 8 years old that fall — The next year
was the ~~#~~ beginning of the great depression and
eventually the Model T was Traded To our
milk man to Cover our milk bill. my Dad could not
Abid debt

=/B
≠ 1938
wrong year
Twas born in 43

In (1948) ~~my Dad~~ purchased a new 1934 Ford
~~I was 16 He learned to drive~~ I was 16 that year
and we learned To drive Together. ~~I have some~~
very pleasant memories of those days.
It gives me pleasure to remember

3½ 2

That was the beginning; by the end of summer he was managing to drive quite well but he always seemed to view the car as an enemy to be conquered.

Labor Day marked the end of summer, School always started the next day. For a treat it was decided that we would all go for a ride in the "Model T" ~~car~~

Sunday in a Dutch Community

~~Holland had about 10,000 people~~
There were about 10,000 people living
in Holland when I was growing
up. The population was about 85%
Dutch adhering to the traditional a
Dutch theology. They called Sunday ~~of the~~
Sabbath and set that day apart to
attend church a.m and p.m. There was
also a Church which held services
in Dutch for the ~~emigrants~~ older people
and immigrants in the community on sun aft
(The Dutch were a people of strong faith
but their beliefs were heavy in
tradition. The rules were rigid –
   1. Children did not play outside on Sunday)
   2. No restaurants would be open on Sunday
   3. No manual labor   ~~7. no Travel except~~
   4. No Shopping   ~~to church.~~
   5. No studying on Sunday
   6. A good Dutch housewife would
       prepare Sunday simple Meals on Saturday
       to be warmed up for Sunday
And on and on it would go
   7. No travel except to services
   8. No Sunday papers – especially the funnies
   9. As circumcision was ordained in the
Old Testament – the Dutch Tradition substituted
Infant baptism instead firmly believing
that was the first step toward salvation
followed by weekly Catacism classes
capped by Confirmation in early Teens
The deed was done

173

My mother was given a Scolfield reference Bible and began to study it in earnest the summer before her 4th child was born foun her ~~feasting on the Acts of the apostles~~ - She ~~followed through on all the cross references~~ and came to a dead standstill when she came Mark 16:16 - Believe and be baptized.

She decided that the new baby would not be baptized. Some one from her ~~the consistory~~ ~~church~~ came to see her and was dumbfounded that she would go against the traditions of the church — They asked her to ~~not~~ Leave the church.

Dream about trying to reach my mom

These are my genes, inherited!
This is the way I am

• but a voice within me struggling
to be heard, says
" you invited me in and that
is not the way I am.

agostic.

Hey! You dizzy dust devil,
Twirling in the sun,
Do you think you're the only one
Having any fun?
Well! I'll dance to my music,
And you can dance to yours,
Just stay from my house,
When I'm out doors.

C.R.B.

✓

Each day of Life is a precious Gift from God.

When I think of Thanksgiving I remember
The first Time I prepared the whole
Thing from start to finish- my guests were
Lil & Hank and their 2 children -
2 weeks ahead- I planned every detail
- It was so exciting To do this in our littl.
house- everything turned out well - Now
this was a major event - I rarely had peop
over - I was scared To death - but felt safe
with my sister.

At last, at last the blizzard ends,
Some rejoice and others lament.
Tattered banners and millions of signs
Go down in history, a new day begins.
The future is a guessing game
Tilted by the strengths and foibles of men
Yet may our words be few but clear
Echoing from our forefathers true and just,
In God --- oh yes,
IN GOD WE TRUST.

Carolyn Ruth Dalman Bouman Baker
October 6, 1922 – July 21, 2017